espionage

espionage

Fascinating stories
of Spies and spying

David Owen

Reader's Digest

The Reader's Digest Association, Inc.
Pleasantville, New York/Montreal

A READER'S DIGEST BOOK

This edition published by The Reader's Digest Association by arrangement with Elwin Street Limited

Conceived and produced by
Elwin Street Limited
Third floor, 144 Liverpool Road
London N1 1LA
United Kingdom
www.elwinstreet.com

FOR READER'S DIGEST
U.S. Project Editors: Barbara Booth, Nancy Shuker
Canadian Project Editor: Pamela Johnson
Associate Art Director: George McKeon
Executive Editor, Trade Publishing: Dolores York
Vice President & Publisher, Trade Publishing: Harold Clarke

Library of Congress Cataloging in Publication Data:

Owen, David, 1939–
    Espionage : fascinating stories of spies and spying / David Owen
        p. cm.
    ISBN 0-7621-0812-6
    1. Espionage. 2. Spies. I. Title
UB270.O88 2006
327.12--dc22   2006043985

Address any comments about *Espionage* to:
    The Reader's Digest Association, Inc.
    Adult Trade Publishing
    Reader's Digest Road
    Pleasantville, NY 10570-7000

For more Reader's Digest products and information, visit our website:
    www.rd.com (in the United States)
    www.readersdigest.ca (in Canada)
    www.readersdigest.co.uk (in the United Kingdom)

Printed in Singapore

1 3 5 7 9 10 8 6 4 2

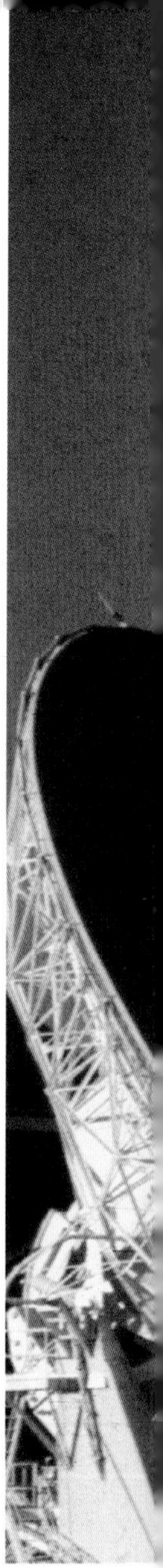

"All warfare is based on deception. There is no place where espionage is not used. Offer the enemy bait to lure him."
—SUN-TZU (~400 B.C.)

Contents

Why Spy?

Spies are fascinating, and their work fuels a million swashbuckling fantasies – taking on a false identity, working undercover in great danger, tracking down vital information, averting attacks, assuring victory. As a craft, espionage opens up a world far removed from everyday routine, with its use of passwords, codes and ciphers, forged papers, dead letter drops, and invisible ink. In a spy's world survival depends on courage, determination and the ability to think quickly on your feet.

Spies have been around since Biblical times. Moses sent them to the Promised Land to explore and report back on the people, the terrain, and the fruitfulness of the land. England's King Alfred the Great used them in the ninth century to find out what the invading Danes were up to. One legend holds that the king took a band of his men disguised as wandering minstrels into the Danish camp. The legend has never been verified, but there is no doubt that the king used intelligence to stay ahead of his foes' every move. Count Baldwin of Flanders, a relative by marriage, provided details of Danish defences. A Flemish monk named Grimbald, a refugee from a monastery sacked by the Norsemen, also became a member of Alfred's team of 'scholarly assistants' – in reality, an expert adviser on the tactics and behaviour of the Danes.

Early trade wars

Five centuries ago the Venetian Republic played a leading role in world trade. It established its power over the eastern Mediterranean by having spies operating all over the territories of its trading rivals. These spies were controlled by a committee named the Council of Ten, which not only ran an efficient secret police force to combat foreign spies on Venetian soil but also developed a code-breaking service that routinely intercepted and read the messages of rival commercial and intelligence organisations. Such success

Spies operate in the shadows, unobserved by the rest of the world.

gave the Republic a huge advantage in undercutting foreign trade and closing off their rivals' attempts to penetrate Venetian intelligence circles. Foreign agents who were successful in gaining useful information were quickly betrayed by their own reports, because these were regularly intercepted and deciphered. The agents were then either arrested or left at large but neutralised with misinformation.

Gunpowder, treason and plot

Over time, spycraft became even more important in survival struggles between nations. In sixteenth-century England, Queen Elizabeth I ruled the greatest Protestant power in an otherwise Roman Catholic Europe, with a navy that threatened the maritime supremacy of the Spanish Empire. This made Elizabeth a prime target for assassination, and a series of plots to replace her with a Catholic ruler were exposed by her highly efficient counterespionage service. One such plot, known as the Babington Plot, eventually led to the execution of Mary, Queen of Scots. A devotee of Mary's, Anthony Babington, recruited a former seminarian named Gilbert Gifford to smuggle letters in and out of Mary's prison, the country estate of Chartley. However, unbeknownst to Babington, Gifford had pledged his allegiance to Sir Francis Walsingham, head of Elizabeth's counterespionage service, and was delivering to him all of Mary's correspondence. This gave Walsingham evidence of Mary's involvement in a plot to assassinate Elizabeth, which he used to persuade Elizabeth that she had no option but to have Mary executed.

Even Elizabeth's successor, James I, was subject to, and survived, a Catholic assassination attempt – the 1605 Gunpowder Plot led by Guy Fawkes, in which a group of provincial English Catholics planned to kill the king, his family, and most of the Protestant aristocracy in one attack by blowing up the Houses of Parliament during the State Opening. However, the plot was foiled due to a tipoff – one of the conspirators had written a letter of warning to one of the Catholic Members of Parliament, Lord Monteagle, who had then warned the secretary of state, Robert Cecil. Recent research has exposed intrigue and counterintrigue, suggesting that government spies recruited the Catholic plotters, planning all along to expose them before the explosion and thus fuel Catholic hatred. So well did they cover their tracks that few people are aware of this today.

A global phenomenon

Espionage has been routinely used by popes, the royal houses of Europe, the leaders of the French and American revolutions and Emperor Napoleon.

There were spies in the English and American civil wars, in the Russian Revolution, in both world wars and during the uneasy decades of the cold war. In fact, throughout history spies have been used to betray hidden entrances to fortresses under siege, to spread alarm and despondency among an enemy to lower its morale and persuade it to surrender, and to gain information on the enemy's situation. From China to India, from the Islamic conquerors who brought their faith to the shores of the Atlantic Ocean to the Golden Horde of the Mongol ruler Genghis Khan, spies have proved an essential tool for victory.

IT'S ALL ABOUT INFORMATION

In the early days, as now, spies dealt mainly in information. As a result, placing your agents deep within the organisation of your adversary – a trading competitor, a rival state or a wartime opponent – could be a genuine advantage. It could help you win commercial and military battles, stiffen defences against hostile attacks and conceal your own weaknesses to make those attacks less likely.

Double agents

On the other hand, your rivals and your enemies were just as likely to mount a similar campaign against your secrets. The more they could find out about your plans, weapons, resources, and objectives, and any weaknesses in your defenses, the more vulnerable you became. In this shadowy world of cat and

(continued on page 14)

Guy Fawkes (third from right) and his coconspirators in the 1605 Gunpowder Plot.

SPYMASTERS & MASTER SPIES
Wilhelm Stieber: Bismarck's Blackmailer

One of the greatest spies and spymasters of the nineteenth century, Wilhelm Stieber, established many features of modern espionage. Born in Merseberg, Germany, in 1818, he studied law in Berlin before working as a criminal lawyer, which led to a position as commissioner in the Berlin criminal police in 1844.

A year later he was sent undercover to report on the emerging Silesian socialist movement. Many activists were jailed on his evidence, and in 1848 he claimed to have rescued the Prussian king, Friedrich Wilhelm IV, from mob attack. He was promoted to director of the Berlin police and sent to London and Paris to report on Karl Marx and the fledgling Communist parties. The information he produced was used at the 1852 international Communist trials in Cologne.

Turning to blackmail

Stieber's method was to entrap his victims and then blackmail them, which brought him powerful enemies, so he depended on the protection of the king. Unfortunately for Stieber, the king was pronounced insane in 1858 and replaced by his brother, later to reign as the first Kaiser of Germany. Stieber was put on trial for blackmail. He insisted he was merely carrying out the orders of the previous monarch, which saved him from jail, but he was sacked and banished from Berlin. For five years he helped the Russians establish their own secret police organisation, then in 1863 met Bismarck, who had the confidence of the new German ruler.

Establishing a secret police

Both men benefitted from the meeting. Stieber's underground contacts alerted him to a death threat aimed at Bismarck, who

subsequently asked him to form a new secret police organisation under the cover name of the Central Intelligence Bureau (CIB). Its first assignment was to gather as much information as possible about Austria, soon to become Bismarck's first target in his campaign for Prussian supremacy in Europe. Stieber toured Austria disguised as a

Cartoon of Count Otto von Bismarck in 1870. Bismarck's use of espionage, in particular his relationship with Wilhelm Stieber, was a key factor in his military victories over Austria and France.

peddler, pushing a cart filled with religious statuettes and crude pornography, a stock in trade intended to appeal to as wide a range of people as possible—including enemy troops. He was therefore able to return to Prussia with priceless data on Austrian strengths, defences and locations of fortifications, all of which helped the Prussians subdue the country in 1866.

Stieber's spywork meant the Germans gained valuable information about French positions in and around Paris, helping them to gain victory in the siege of 1870–71. This map shows the positions of the French (in red) and German (in black) troops during the siege.

Building a spy network

Bismarck's next target was France, which was invaded and conquered in 1870–71. For this much tougher assignment, Stieber saturated the country with his own spies. He was said to know the location of every farm, village and house in the proposed fighting area. He had legions of spies in place in Paris before the city fell under siege, and more than 9,000 spies were said to be reporting to German headquarters in Versailles alone by the time France capitulated.

One of Stieber's greatest coups of the Franco-Prussian war came during the peace negotiations at Versailles. When Jules Favre, the French minister of foreign affairs, arrived at Versailles, he was met by a coachman who was in fact a German spy. Favre was taken to lodge in the house that Stieber was using as the headquarters of his spy network, and Stieber himself was recommended to him as a valet. In this role, Stieber was able to go through his 'master's' pockets and despatch cases on a daily basis, collecting valuable data and information that he passed on to Bismarck to aid him in his negotiations.

King of sleuth-hounds

Stieber's Bureau was greatly expanded after the wars. He succeeded in establishing new ideas on espionage and counterespionage, including manipulating the press, business and banks; the use of terrorism and honey traps (lures to trap criminals); military censorship and psychological warfare; and the saturation of a target area with spies to ensure multiple channels of information. He even established a police-run brothel where government officials and foreign diplomats were entertained by high-class prostitutes, all of whom reported to the CIB. He also ran overseas agents in Paris, Vienna and London.

Though Bismarck respected him and called him his 'king of sleuth-hounds', he was never accepted in society because of his use of blackmail, and in later years his name was largely ignored. He died in 1882, all but forgotten, despite laying the foundations of modern espionage. In particular, he insisted that large spy networks were needed to produce a complete picture, and that having a "multiplicity of spies" would avoid becoming victim to deliberate disinformation – methods that are still standard today.

mouse, perhaps the most dangerous figure is the double agent – the spy with divided loyalties or personal greed who trades information between contenders and who betrays both sides with equal ease.

To win an espionage battle, a spy organisation must not only support and monitor the efforts of its own agents but also be aware of the efforts of opposition spies on its own territory. As a result, the development of espionage has been a never-ending battle between spy and counterspy. Wherever spies have tried to bury themselves deep in an opponent's army, company or society, counterintelligence forces have to watch for the telltale signs of someone who does not quite belong, who shows too much interest in sensitive places or pieces of information, who associates with people who may already be suspect, or whose background details seem less than convincing.

Difficulties of hidden identities

Other problems frustrate the efforts of even the most professional and successful espionage agents:

- Spies must be protected from those on their own side who might betray their existence through indiscretion or treachery.

- Their own paymasters usually must follow a policy of denying a spy's existence if operations go wrong and an agent is captured.

- Because spies are unidentified even to those on their own side, the information they provide may never reach the people who need it most, or it may not be taken seriously.

- In cases where information is circulated to the right people, it may be discounted. The shady reputation of undercover organisations has often led to their efforts being underrated and unappreciated, leading to catastrophic mistakes and opportunities missed.

RECENT DEVELOPMENTS

There have been marked changes in the espionage world in our own times, from the closing decades of the twentieth century to the present day. These changes are due to a number of factors, including the development of new techniques—needed to face the new challenges and political landscape of the modern world and the role of espionage within that world—as well as the availability of new technology.

Specialisation

Placing effective human agents, working from patriotic motives or deep personal convictions, into a society as closed and secretive as the Soviet Union at the height of the Cold War was hugely difficult. As a result, greater emphasis was put on technical intelligence, such as electronic and photographic surveillance, signals intelligence (the interception of foreign signals—from Morse code to missile testing), traffic analysis (the study of patterns in the flow of communications), communications interception (from listening in to radio broadcasts to phone tapping) and code and cipher cracking.

Criminal damage

In the West, spies were increasingly subject to restrictions and limitations of their freedom of action imposed by their own side. At a time when espionage activities by the former Soviet bloc appeared to be safely in decline, the Clinton administration in the United States barred the CIA from recruiting any agents with criminal records. Furthermore, agents and their controllers were warned they would be held liable for any damage done as a result of their operations. But the fact remains that during the long history of espionage, criminals have often made excellent agents due to their experience in evading authority and their wide networks of contacts on the fringes of society.

The destruction of the World Trade Centre in New York by terrorists in 2001 announced the emergence of a new and far more deadly adversary outside the old Cold War battle lines. Today's terrorists operate in tightly regulated cells involving small numbers of people operating in secret and, as a result, are in some ways less vulnerable to technical intelligence than the Soviet bloc used to be. The need for human agents able to penetrate their networks has never been higher.

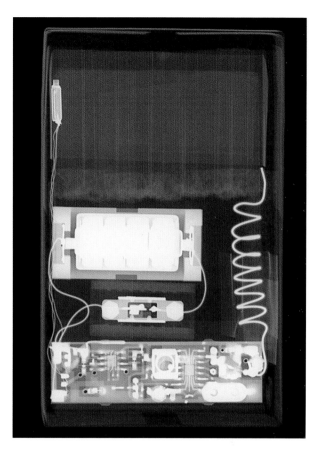

X-ray image revealing an audio transmitter hidden in a cigarette packet, which could be used for covert surveillance or espionage.

Power games

A final important change has been a shift in emphasis in how spies are seen by those who use them, as well as by those who suffer from the spies of the opposing sides. This has shifted from an overwhelmingly negative image to a much more objective and positive one. Not all spies are simply villains, working away at the foundations of the defences – of a nation, an army, or a company – to seize a fatal advantage. In recent times they have often been able to help defuse tension and make surprise attacks less likely, especially in the uneasy balance of terror that governed relations between the superpower blocs of the East and the West during the Cold War. For example, the whole theory of the nuclear deterrent depended not only on both sides knowing that an attack on the opposition would result in an instant and overwhelming retaliation, but in their knowing that the other side was aware of that balance too. As weapons became increasingly destructive, the role of the intelligence agent became ever more vital in defusing the danger that this fearful weapon might be launched by accident, or through fear of an opposing attack.

If, for example, the Soviet Union had made a move to sound alarms in Western circles, then only the spies were likely to have access to information that might reveal the real intentions, and capabilities, of the Eastern bloc. Very often the threat might be an illusion fed by paranoia or the need to reassure their subject populations that their defences were strong: If the real resources that could be deployed to make the threat genuine simply did not exist, then that very knowledge would help ensure that the West did not overreact and escalate their own threats in turn.

The presence of agents on one another's soil therefore provided extra warning. Should the unthinkable ever have happened, with the launching of ballistic missiles in a preemptive strike, the four-minute warning between those launchings being detected and the first warheads detonating over their targets would provide time only for the reflex firing of the return strike. However, if either side could see how genuine levels of tension, fear or readiness were changing on a day-to-day basis, as opposed to political posturing for different reasons, then this period of warning could be greatly extended. This would allow extra time for talks, for negotiations or for stronger defences to be deployed to deter the action before it began. And where terrorist threats are concerned, every time a plot or conspiracy is uncovered, innocent lives are spared.

(continued on page 21)

TECHNOLOGY
Airplanes make way for satellites

Satellite surveillance means that governments now have unlimited access to the activities of other countries.

Aeroplanes can fly across a continent in a matter of hours and carry out all kinds of intelligence gathering on their journey, from detailed photographs to electronic eavesdropping. While these reconnaissance missions can be carried out with impunity only in wartime conditions – and even then can be interrupted or frustrated by the other side's fighters, anti-aircraft fire or surface-to-air missiles – carrying out missions in peacetime becomes subject to myriad legal restrictions and prohibitions over the sovereignty of a country's airspace.

Satellites encounter no such obstacles. Their orbits place them well beyond retaliation, free to cover every part of the world in the greatest detail. Ever more sophisticated sensors allow them to watch out for troop movements or missile launches, new fortifications or weapons plants, new missile launchers or new warships.

For the first time in the long history of espionage, every detail of another country's security backyard lies open to the scrutiny of experts. This presents an enormous opportunity: Since satellites operate on a continuous basis rather than relying on a single snapshot of a particular area of the world at a specific time, changes and attempts at camouflage can be spotted.

SPYMASTERS & MASTER SPIES
Blinker Hall and Von Rintelen

The Royal Navy's Director of Intelligence (DNI) in World War I was Captain Reginald 'Blinker' Hall (so called on account of a persistent facial tic that caused high-speed blinking). His first espionage coup had been carried out on a 1908 visit to the German naval base of Kiel in command of the training cruiser HMS *Cornwall*. He had been asked to check the number of shipbuilding slipways the Germans had built on part of the base out of bounds to visitors, so he borrowed a motorboat from a British Duke also visiting Kiel, and after changing into a yachting blazer and white flannels, took it for a series of high-speed runs up and down the harbour. He managed to engineer a breakdown that left the boat helpless opposite the new slipways. By the time help arrived, two of his officers, hidden in the launch's cabin, had photographed every detail of the construction.

Gathering information

Within months of the outbreak of war, he was able to read all the principal German naval and diplomatic codes, thanks to three pieces of astonishing good luck. On 26 August 1914, the German warship *Magdeburg* ran aground on a sandbank on the island of Odensholm, off the coast of Estonia. In response to her signals, a large German torpedo boat was ordered to rescue the crew and the secret papers on board. Oddly, when it became clear that the rescue vessel would have to make two trips, the papers were left on board with the captain and 57 of his crew. Before the torpedo boat could return to take them off, two Russian cruisers arrived and collected the lot. The Russians offered the codebook to the British, who sent a cruiser to collect it, and it was delivered to Hall on 13 October.

Seven weeks later a trawler fishing in the North Sea found a wooden chest in its nets, which had been thrown overboard from a German destroyer sunk in a skirmish with the Royal Navy off the Dutch coast. When opened, this was found to contain the codes used by German admirals to communicate with German consulates overseas. Finally, the German merchant ship code was seized from a German-Australian steamer by a Royal Australian Navy boarding party on 26 October.

As a result, Hall knew about all the major movements of the German High Seas Fleet from the end of 1914 to the end of the war.

Von Rintelen, the German naval captain imprisoned in the United States for planning acts of sabotage during World War I.

Sadly, as is so often the case with high-quality intelligence, the chief problem was convincing others of its reliability. The Battle of Jutland presented the British Navy with an opportunity to inflict a crippling defeat on the enemy, which it missed because of uncertainty over the German positions.

However, Hall's team had forecast the German battle fleet's preparations a week before they actually sailed. It had positive information that the German ships had left harbour, before the enemy had even reached the open sea. Later, when both fleets were searching for one another, Hall's team knew the precise position of the German warships. This potentially battle-winning information never reached Admiral Jellicoe, commander of the Grand Fleet. Henry Oliver, Hall's predecessor as DNI, and Captain Thomas Jackson, the Admiralty's director of operations, insisted Room 40's information was wrong and did not pass the details to Jellicoe.

Von Rintelen

One of Hall's opposite numbers was a German naval captain named Von Rintelen, who suffered even more severely from suspicious colleagues. He spoke fluent English and was sent to the United States in 1915 to cooperate with the German military attaché, Franz Von Papen, in organising a campaign of sabotage against industry and shipping to prevent war material reaching the Allies.

Von Papen, German military attaché to the United States during World War I thwarted Von Rintelen's plans for sabotage.

The diplomat was horrified by Von Rintelen's bold plans and his development of weapons such as bombs triggered by the revolutions of a ship's propellers, and a crude timing device made from a thin sheet of copper separating sulfuric and picric acids (when the sulfuric acid corroded its way through the copper, the two ingredients mixed and the bomb exploded). Von Papen and his commercial attaché, Heinrich Albert, had plans for much more subtle disruption, and although Von Rintelen afterward claimed to have been responsible for the disappearance of a number of American merchant ships, this was not confirmed. On the other hand, Von Papen convinced Berlin of his worries, and Von Rintelen was recalled to Germany.

A passage was booked on board a neutral Dutch steamer, which was to call at Southampton en route to mainland Europe. The signals were read by Hall's team, and a naval guard was put on board the ship when it docked in England. Von Rintelen was arrested and later extradited to the United States, where he was imprisoned in Atlanta for the rest of the war – for planning, rather than actually carrying out, sabotage. Ironically, on his release he returned to England, where he applied for British citizenship.

ESPIONAGE IN ACTION
The great World War I invasion scare

Blinker Hall twice became a victim of the security walls between espionage organisations and those responsible for normal military operations. In 1915 his team used their mastery of German ciphers to persuade the enemy to waste time and resources laying mines in part of the North Sea not used by British shipping. Unfortunately, the operations branch had not told them they planned to route the cruiser HMS *Hampshire*, carrying Secretary of State for War Lord Kitchener on a visit to Russia, through that area. The ship hit a mine and sank, and Kitchener drowned.

The second occasion came in the fall of 1916 when the British and French armies on the Western front were hard-pressed by German attacks. Hall decided to make the enemy scale down their operations by threatening them with a possible Allied landing behind German lines on the coast of northern Belgium. His trump card was his secret emergency war code, which he had developed the year before and planted on the Germans so they would accept it as genuine.

He had sent an agent to Rotterdam with a copy of the code in an official dispatch case to stay at a hotel known to be watched by German agents. One evening he asked the hall porter's advice on the local nightlife before leaving for the evening, with the dispatch case left unlocked but hidden beneath a spare suit of clothes in his room. He found a hiding place facing the hotel and was delighted to see the light in his room switched on after half an hour. He reasoned that the Germans would want to return the codebook after photographing it to avoid giving their theft away. So he waited for another three hours and saw the light come on again while the book was replaced.

Later Hall added further information to reassure the Germans of the value of their find. He sent a series of signals containing genuine but low-grade information using the code. After intercepting genuine German signals, it became clear that they had no suspicions that the code was false.

The code was then used to suggest invasion plans to the Germans. Several urgent signals were sent about forces of flat-bottomed barges and coastal bombardment vessels assembling in Harwich and Dover and in the Thames Estuary. Hall next had a dozen copies of the edition of the *Daily Mail* for 12 September 1916, printed with an extra paragraph in the late news 'Stop Press' section. Some of these were partially blanked out, as though spotted by the censor, but it was still possible to read about 'Great Military Preparations'. These doctored editions of the newspaper were left in places where they were likely to attract the attention of German agents.

Lord Kitchener in a World War I army recruitment poster.

Unforeseen consequences

The evidence soon showed that the plan had succeeded all too well. British agents in the occupied part of Belgium soon began reporting massive German troop movements toward the north Belgian coast, and a reciprocal invasion scare began in England. Because Hall's campaign had been secret, he couldn't reveal what had happened, and there was always a faint chance that these enemy reinforcements were part of a genuine German plan to invade England that owed nothing to his deception. So the tension increased, trenches were dug, fortifications were built along the threatened stretches of the British coast and plans were drawn up for the evacuation of the civilian population in the area. After an agonising wait, it eventually became clear that both sides were similarly waiting for the enemy to act, and invasion fears subsided.

Technology as key

New technical developments in intelligence gathering are far removed from the classic human agent associated with the world of empires, monarchies and the Cold War. In fact, espionage has become far more sophisticated, more complex and more powerful in the modern world. Human agents still have an important role to play, but are today supported by a whole range of equipment, from satellites to remotely piloted aircraft, from infrared scans to radar that can see halfway around the world, from the analysis of signals traffic to the reading of radio messages and even e-mails. As technology continues to develop at breathtaking speed, no doubt the world of espionage will adapt to include ever more ingenious methods of finding out information.

However, such is the double-edged nature of espionage and intelligence work: if anyone is clever enough, original enough and painstaking enough to make disinformation fit with what can be seen from space, there is far less chance of that data ever being discredited, representing a truly tempting target for counterintelligence agents and organisations. This means that agents must constantly question the reliability of their sources and decide what can and cannot be trusted. With information becoming more plentiful, more varied and more detailed, the world of espionage has become more challenging – and more important.

Electronic and photographic surveillance plays an increasingly important role in espionage as technological developments provide human agents with an ever-growing range of resources and backup.

Types of Espionage

While espionage has undergone many changes over the years, they have been mainly tactical, and the overall objective has remained the same: to discover the secrets of potential enemies before they can do any harm. Today the major differences lie in the wider scope of information that spies seek to uncover and the technology they use. And, more than ever before, commercial and trade intelligence is playing a greater part as companies seek to erode one another's competitive advantage.

In the past, spies were limited to what they could see and hear – information gathered from contacts, documents they stole or copied, or details they could remember. Since then, technology has transformed the capabilities of the spy with the addition of miniature cameras, photocopiers disguised as pens – able to copy documents simply by rolling over them – sensitive microphones to pick up and record conversations, and satellites that survey the entire globe. While these technological advances have revolutionised the world of espionage, they have not rendered human spies obsolete. They may have altered the ways in which spies work, but there are still some areas where good old-fashioned human intelligence is still vital.

Technical intelligence

Radio signals, coded communications, recorded conversations, intercepted calls and e-mails, satellite surveillance and electronic monitoring of ship and aircraft movements all contribute to increasingly complex intelligence pictures. Thanks to developments in the world of technology, it is now possible to monitor everything, from the development of weapons of mass destruction to the progress of nuclear capability, from monitoring compliance with arms-reduction treaties to warning of the deployment of new forces in politically and socially tense areas. These important types of technical intelligence are covered in later chapters.

Satellites are an increasingly important information-gathering tool in the world of espionage.

A mini spy camera from the 1950s – one of the earliest technological tools available to human agents.

Human intelligence

In some areas of espionage, however, human agents are still the best information source because only they can supply the missing factors – the intentions of those in command. For example, Saddam Hussein had forces capable of invading Kuwait long before 2 August 1990, but no one knew where and when the blow would fall. Technical intelligence is of no use in this kind of situation, because only human espionage can reveal the way opposing leaders think – what they know, what they want and what they plan to do to attain their objectives.

Commercial and trade intelligence

As the danger of world war recedes, civilian espionage has become more prominent. National interests are now more focused on economic strength and commercial competition. Information regarding the strategy of a competitor is invaluable and is often used as a tool when negotiating contracts with overseas customers.. Details of new technologies are as vital to economic espionage as information on new weapons is to the military.

One of the most famous examples of industrial espionage involves French company Aérospatiale's Concorde and Russia's supersonic jet, the Tu-144. Sergei Pavlov, who was officially representing Aeroflot (Russia's national airline) in France, was arrested in 1965 and found to be in possession of detailed plans of Concorde's braking system, landing gear, and airframe. Sergei Fabiew, another agent, arrested in 1977, was believed to have obtained the entire plans for the prototype Concorde in the mid-'60s. There were certainly many superficial similarities between Concorde and the Tu-144, but there were dramatic differences between their respective control, navigation and engine systems. This is because the information the two Russian agents obtained covered early development plans, so Soviet engineers could not copy the final design. Instead, the information could serve only as a general indication of the work of the Concorde design team.

HUMAN AGENTS IN ACTION

Nothing demonstrates the importance of on-the-ground agents in gathering intelligence more than Soviet espionage during the building of the American atomic bomb. A band of their spies enabled the USSR. to explode its own atom bomb only four years after the United States detonated the first one. How they did it is a classic case of spies in action.

It's all about networking

The story begins in London in 1933 with the arrival of a 57-year-old German émigré, Rene Kuczinski, a Jewish Communist who had fled the country when the Nazis came to power. An eminent economist, Kuczinski took up a post at the London School of Economics. He already had ties to Soviet intelligence before his arrival in the U.K., but he engaged in espionage mainly to support his children, Jurgen and Ruth, who soon began recruiting agents to spy for the Russians.

They first made contact with another German refugee, a physicist named Klaus Fuchs, who would later move to America to join the atomic bomb project. Ruth had already set up radio communications with her Moscow contacts while living an outwardly ordinary suburban life with her husband, Leon Buerton, a British veteran of the Spanish Civil War, and her two children. She controlled several important agents, including Melita Norwood, who worked for the British end of the atomic bomb project as

British scientist Dr Alan Nunn May passed details of the atomic bomb project to the Russians.

personal secretary to the director. Top-secret information crossed her desk on a daily basis and she provided the Soviets with a steady stream of quality information.

MI5 first suspected Ruth in 1947, but when agents visited her home, she played the role of housewife and mother to perfection, giving nothing away. She therefore managed to avoid capture. Nevertheless, she and her family fled to East Germany because she was convinced MI5 would return to arrest her. Once back in the Eastern bloc, the Communist authorities awarded her two Orders of the Red Banner and made her an honorary colonel in the Soviet Army in recognition of her espionage work.

Meanwhile, Russian agent Igor Gouzenko, who defected in Ottawa in September 1945, identified a British scientist inside the atomic bomb programme as a former member of the Communist party and a Soviet spy. Dr Alan Nunn May had worked in Montreal, and Gouzenko knew the scientist had sent the Russians small samples of the uranium used for the bombs. He had returned to his work in Britain, but the Canadians informed the British of his treachery, and he was promptly arrested. He claimed at his trial that when he passed the information along, Russia had been allied with Britain and the United States, and that he was acting for the overall safety of mankind, but the court refused to accept his defence. He was given a ten-year jail term.

This was the tip of the iceberg. Gouzenko knew there were more Soviet spies with access to the secrets of the atomic bomb project, but they appeared in his records only as code names. The code was eventually cracked when Soviet diplomatic radio signals were deciphered under the Venona program (see pages 144–45). Klaus Fuchs, by then back in Britain and working at the Harwell nuclear research facility in Oxfordshire, was the first to be exposed. Fuchs initially denied any involvement in espionage, and at first the intelligence services did not have enough evidence to charge him. However, after repeated questioning, he eventually confessed on January 23, 1950.

Uncovering the network

Fuchs himself provided leads to others in the network. His courier, who relayed information to the Russians, was code-named 'Raymond'. Fuchs never knew his real name, but did produce a rough description. A former Soviet agent, the American Elizabeth Bentley (see page 83), provided more information after admitting her involvement with Russian spy networks. She divulged the names of several agents who worked for Abraham Brothman, an engineering firm based in the New York borough of Queens. One of them closely matched Fuchs's description of 'Raymond': a Swiss immigrant named Harry Gold. Gold was arrested and questioned. He admitted that on a trip to Santa Fe to collect information from Fuchs, he had also stopped in Albuquerque *(continued on page 31)*

Harry Gold was betrayed by Klaus Fuchs as Raymond – the courier who delivered his information about the atomic bomb project to the Russians.

SPYMASTERS & MASTER SPIES
Civil War Spies in Long Skirts

It was once believed that female agents were less capable than men of gaining access to valuable information. The truth was very different: Their perceived remoteness made them formidable spies as early as the American Civil War, where many proved so successful they became renowned.

For example, Elizabeth Van Lew, a member of a slave-owning family in Richmond, Virginia, was born in the North and was a Union sympathizer. She feigned eccentricity (and subsequently became known as 'Crazy Bet') as a cover for her Northern espionage activities. She visited Northern prisoners to obtain details of the Confederate units and defences they had seen on the way to their prison camps. She also ran escape lines to help fleeing Northern prisoners reach their own lines – couriers passed her information back to the Northern commanders.

Her greatest coup: She placed a slave her family had freed, Mary Bowser, in Confederate president Jefferson Davis's household. Mary pretended to be illiterate, although she could read and write very well. She read every document she could find and passed vital information along to the North.

Confederate spies

The South had its female spies too: among them, Belle Boyd and Rose Greenhow. When the war started, Belle Boyd returned to her birthplace in Martinsburg, Virginia, and reported to Southern commanders the movements of the approaching

Northern forces. She was arrested and questioned by Alan Pinkerton of Northern counterintelligence, but in 1862 she was released to live with her aunt in Front Royal. When the town was taken by Northern troops, she crossed back to the Southern lines to report that it was lightly held and ripe for recapture. Acting on her information, the

Belle Boyd's espionage work for the Confederates helped the South recapture Front Royal during the American Civil War.

Northern troops attacking Confederate cavalrymen in the first Battle of Bull Run, 21 July 1861. Information gained from the Confederate spy Rose Greenhow helped Southern troops to win the battle.

South did in fact recapture the town and vital nearby bridges. Once again she was captured and questioned, and once again she was released to return home. Her final mission was to London to rally British support for the flagging Confederate cause.

Rose Greenhow helped bring about the first and most dramatic Southern victory at the Battle of Bull Run in 1861. Before the outbreak of war, she was a prominent hostess in Washington society. She remained in the capital and communicated with the Confederacy through a network of couriers, passing on gossip from her social gatherings. Betty Duval, one of her couriers, carried coded messages hidden in her thick dark hair giving the route and timings of the Northern advance from Washington to Manassas, along the Bull Run stream. The Confederate general, Pierre Beauregard, used her information to outmanoeuvre the Northern forces and win the battle.

A month later Rose was picked up by Pinkerton's counterespionage teams, arrested and imprisoned. Once released, she sailed to Europe to be presented to Queen Victoria and the French emperor Napoleon III. On her return to the United States, her ship ran aground off the coast. She tried to reach land in a small rowing boat but was drowned when it capsized. Critics, scornful of the book she had written on her exploits, insisted she had drowned because of the gold bars she carried in her clothing!

to meet David Greenglass, a soldier working on the Manhattan Project, whose regular courier was ill. Greenglass's sister Ethel had married Julius Rosenberg, a Communist Party member already in touch with Soviet intelligence, and Greenglass asked him to pass on sensitive material to the Soviets.

Rosenberg was arrested on 17 July 1950, the last one of the group to be seized. While all of the other agents admitted supplying atomic bomb secrets to the Russians, the Rosenbergs maintained their innocence. Ironically, they were the only ones executed for treason. The others had bargained for their lives with the authorities. The Venona material was too sensitive to use in evidence at their trial, but when it was later made public, their guilt was confirmed beyond any reasonable doubt.

The explosive success of human agents
Before the Soviet espionage network was uncovered, it had given the Russians enough information to build and detonate their first atomic bomb in September 1949.

The Americans learned the awful truth almost immediately. US aircraft could measure the proportion of plutonium particles in the upper atmosphere. A sudden increase in plutonium demonstrated that a nuclear bomb had exploded a week or so before – and it could only have been one built by Russia.

The Russians alleged that the spies had made little difference and that they had developed the bomb on their own. However, Molotov and Khruschev would later admit that the information from the spies concerning the American atomic bomb project, code-named Enormoz by the Russians, had greatly simplified and accelerated the development of Russia's first atomic weapons. This was because it allowed them to avoid dangerous tests to determine the size of the critical mass of the bomb, which had consumed a good deal of time during the American project and claimed at least two lives.

Furthermore, Lavrenti Beria, head of Stalin's KGB, knew that failure to develop the atomic bomb would mean his execution. He therefore gave the atomic bomb project the highest possible status of national security and ordered those working on the project to make an exact copy of the second American bomb (the plutonium bomb that destroyed the Japanese city of Nagasaki) as soon as possible since it clearly worked. The first Soviet bomb copied many features of the US weapon, even down to the bolts used to assemble it.

FBI agents escorting Julius Rosenberg, a 32-year-old engineer who was involved in the Venona spy network, into the FBI building on 17 July 1950.

Types of Espionage

SPYMASTERS & MASTER SPIES
Mata Hari and the Beautiful Blonde of Antwerp

Throughout the first 'Golden Age' of spying, before and during World War I, some individual agents became legends. Others, not so well known, however, achieved much more. For example, the German agent Maria de Victoria, daughter of General Baron Hans von Kretschman and Baroness Jennie von Gustedt, was an accomplished linguist and went to work for the German Secret Service in 1910.

She married Manuel Gustave Victoria, an Argentine later arrested by the French in 1917 for spying. By then, the British had been chasing his wife for three years. She was finally tracked down by the US Army's Cipher Bureau, which cracked her coded messages.

She was arrested on 27 April 1918, charged with espionage, and found guilty of importing explosives for sabotage purposes, including an attempt to block the Panama Canal. She died in prison two years later.

Mata Hari
On the other hand, Mata Hari, one of the most notorious names in espionage history, achieved very little. She claimed to be the daughter of a Dutch sailor and a Javanese temple dancer, learning exotic dancing from her mother and taking the name 'Mata Hari', or 'Eye of the Dawn' in Javanese. In reality, she was born Margaretha Zelle in 1876, daughter of a hatter from Leeuwarden. In 1894 she married John MacLeod and went with him to the Dutch East Indies. After eight years the marriage broke up, and in 1902 she returned to Holland. She then danced in nightclubs in Berlin and Holland. During World War I she aroused the suspicions of the French, who claimed she had betrayed Allied spies to the Germans and passed sensitive information to them through neutral diplomatic channels. By 1916 she was in Madrid, with clients in both the French and German embassies. The French claimed that the Germans had sent a ciphered signal to Berlin – a cipher the French had broken – requesting additional funds for their agent H21, whom the French had identified as Mata Hari.

Since the French claimed the Germans knew that their code had been broken, it is

Exotic dancer Mata Hari was suspected of acting as a double agent during World War I.

The execution of Mata Hari at Vincennes, near Paris, on 15 October 1917, on suspicion of passing information to the Germans during World War I.

possible that Berlin sacrificed her to protect another, more successful, agent or because the Germans suspected her of being a double agent. In any event, they ordered her to Paris to pick up her money. The French promptly arrested her. Their only real evidence? She had accepted 30,000 marks from a German officer. She insisted it was payment for her favours, but the French thought the sum too large and found her guilty. She was shot by firing squad on 15 October 1917.

Dr. Elisabeth Schragmueller

Much more formidable was the woman who trained her. Ironically, Dr. Elisabeth Schragmueller was a much more formidable woman. She had pioneered the concept of sacrificing an agent to protect a more valuable spy. While working at the University of Freiburg in 1914, she wrote to Walther Nicolai, head of German military intelligence, asking for a job. He posted her to a military censorship team in German-occupied Belgium, where her linguistic gifts and aptitude for intelligence work were noted quickly. After training in Baden-Baden, she was transferred to a newly established German spy school in Antwerp, where she developed a new and more objective approach to espionage.

She encouraged agents to force contacts to visit them, putting the contact under greater psychological pressure and making them more liable to betray falsehoods and reveal information. Formidably intelligent, with a strong personality, striking appearance and mesmerising blue eyes, she was known to her opponents by reputation as 'Fraulein Doktor' or the 'Beautiful Blonde of Antwerp'. After Germany's defeat, she became a professor of history at the University of Munich. She died in 1940 at the age of fifty-three.

Human Agents

Human agents are still the backbone of worldwide espionage. And how they find the information they need and pass it back to their controllers still depends on a perfect cover and a reliable spy network. Recruiting agents, developing and sticking to a cover story and avoiding capture are all vital, as is knowing what to do when the worst happens.

Agents are constantly in danger of exposure because of the contacts they have to make. An agent sent into a target country from outside most likely will not have direct access to needed intelligence. His or her usefulness therefore depends on recruiting good subagents who not only have access to valuable information, but are willing to steal it.

This makes a recruiting agent extremely vulnerable. Every potential subagent may, in fact, be a double agent, placed in the recruiter's way as a deliberate trap. And recruited subagents may betray themselves – and the recruiter – with simple mistakes. Subagents may have to switch sides to survive. Double agents can, of course, open up channels for disinformation, but they can also put an entire network of agents within their own country at risk.

It was once common for spies to operate as part of a diplomatic mission. Even now defence and commercial attachés are usually able to build up contacts with local people who supply them with all kinds of important information in the course of their diplomatic duties. For more sensitive data they – like their diplomatic predecessors – must run agents to gather information rather than act as spies themselves.

The advantage of a diplomatic position is that it carries diplomatic immunity. If diplomats' espionage activities are unmasked, the worst punishment they face is expulsion from the country. A disadvantage for

Despite the development of new technologies that allow espionage from a distance, human agents seeking out information in the field are still a vital part of any spy network.

diplomats is their high profile. Diplomats will be watched very closely whenever they venture outside the embassy, and the contacts they make among the local population will come under immediate suspicion and be carefully noted.

COVER STORIES AND CAMOUFLAGE

For protection a spy needs a solid identity and cover story – real enough to be convincing and simple enough for the person to maintain it under lengthy interrogation. If a spy is stopped and questioned by the authorities as part of a general check, a solid cover story will often deflect suspicion. Wherever possible, covers are close to the truth so that it is easier for the spy to remember the details – the agent's age and place of birth, family background and work experience in a particular trade, for example, will be left unchanged. Only recent personal data such as name, address and the reason for being in the country have to be changed for protection. Sometimes, if an

Documents used by Yugoslavian spy and British double agent Duskov Popov to back up his cover stories.

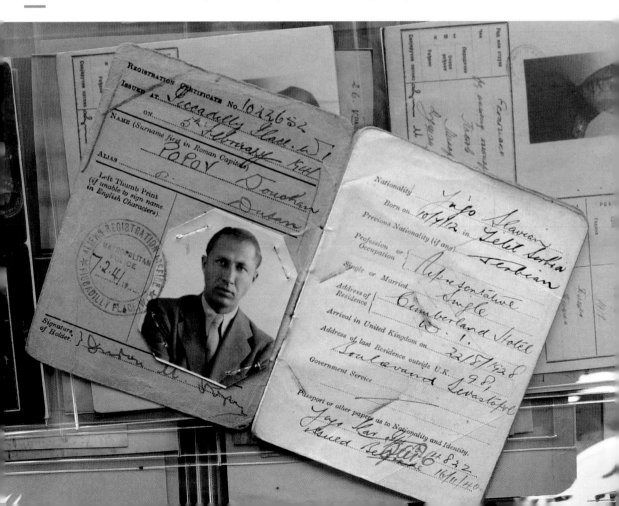

agent's identity is not known to the enemy, he or she can operate under his or her own name.

Stolen identities

If truthful backgrounds give away too much, agents may use cover stories based on real people. This has the advantage of official records confirming personal details, but the disadvantage of the agents possibly running into someone who knows the adopted person. Even more dangerous, the adopted person might be under suspicion with the authorities for an entirely different reason – embezzling or missing child-support payments, for example. Detailed questioning of the agent could easily reveal fatal gaps in the cover story.

Fictitious identities

Making up an identity and cover story is a safer option. Even here, however, the agent should stick closely to the details of his or her real life, especially in the skills or experience they claim as part of the cover. The cover story has to be respectable, offering no hint of being linked to clandestine work, and agents have to learn the most recent details of their stories particularly well, since these are the ones to which authorities pay the greatest attention.

Occasionally, an agent may have to use more than one identity and cover story, but this is a double-edged weapon. Apart from the danger of confusing the details between one persona and the other, anyone who is carrying two sets of identity papers when they are searched might as well have the word 'spy' tattooed on his or her forehead.

FORMULA FOR A SUCCESSFUL SPY

What makes a successful spy? Such a person must be able to blend into any background – for recruiting subagents or gathering information. The spy also needs to be confident, able to start a conversation easily and break the ice in any social situation. Further, he or she must be adept at getting people to talk about themselves, their backgrounds and their work – without realizing they are being questioned.

Observation

A good spy must be observant and able to recall details from even the briefest glimpse of complex equipment or technical documents. Sometimes a second sighting of a particular car or a familiar face, clothes or walk might be the only warning a spy has that he or she is being tailed. Agents in occupied Europe during World War II were on the alert for the smell of genuine coffee. Only the Germans and the criminal black marketeers had real coffee, so its odour guaranteed the presence of someone in close contact with the German authorities or the criminal black market.

Blending in

Sometimes undercover agents are drawn from the local community so that they have the right accent, use the correct idioms and know what subjects are acceptable – and unacceptable – in conversation. During the Northern Ireland emergency, agents were familiar enough with the territory, its people and the local dialects that they could sense how far they could successfully go with questioning.

Convincing the enemy

A spy cannot always pass as a native, however, particularly in a closed or secretive society. The only alternative is to have a convincing cover story to account for one's presence, and give local people an incentive to make contact. This saves the need to mimic local accents and intonations. Selling or servicing farm machinery, for example, with the right skills and help from the company producing the equipment, gives a convincing reason to be in the area. Carrying out the job efficiently can eventually lead to a degree of acceptance.

Finding and recruiting sources

Once in hostile territory, an agent must depend on sources or subagents, just as a police detective uses informers to find out about planned crimes in the area. In many cases agents must find and recruit their own people within the country to gain specific information. The foreign agent must persuade subagents to overcome their natural loyalties. Sources are usually classified as 'primary' or 'access'. Primary sources have direct contact with the information the agent is seeking. Access sources lack this direct contact but have 'access' to primary sources – reducing the risks involved with the agent undertaking this task.

Spotting a likely prospect

There are certain categories of people who are more likely to be persuaded to turn on the country in which they live. These include people who defected to the new country and have become disillusioned with it, as well as people with a grudge against the political system. Other categories of potential spies are greedy people who can be bought, and people who can be compelled to cooperate by threats to family back home, blackmail or other ugly means.

Drawing them in

The first meeting with a potential source or subagent is the most dangerous, so the agent needs to keep the cover story as convincing as possible. Initial requests for information should be casual, such as acting as an engineer or contractor wanting to find business contacts in the new country. This low-level information may be rewarded with profuse thanks, small payments, and gifts.

Over time the requests for information can touch on more sensitive issues, with rewards increasing in proportion. The critical point is the changeover from publicly available information to confidential material. The agent may need to offer extra inducements to overcome the doubts of the potential subagent. It may be enough to point out how much the source has already been paid to produce information, betray his country and employers, and the highly vulnerable position he or she now occupies. Alternatively, the agent may pretend that the information is not very important in an attempt to persuade the source to continue collecting the rewards. One common ploy is to explain that the information merely confirms what the agent already knew and is therefore much less important than it seems.

The wartime identity papers of Nancy Wake, an Australian spy who performed undercover espionage work in France for the Allies during World War II.

RECRUITING SOURCES AND SUBAGENTS IN WARTIME

During World War II the British goverment charged the Special Operations Executive (SOE) with mounting espionage and sabotage operations against the enemy in Nazi-occupied countries. They operated in several countries including Poland, Belgium, the Netherlands, Yugoslavia, and Denmark, but were particularly active in helping the French Resistance. In an effort to maximise their chances of success, the organisation gave agents a checklist to help them recruit sources and subagents in hostile territory. Those who hated their occupiers were obvious targets for cooperation, but there was still the very real and dangerous possibility that they were undercover enemy sympathisers.

Assessing potential sources

Agents were told to sum up each potential source's motivation for spy work before approaching them. Common incentives included hatred of those in power, a desire to hasten the occupiers' downfall or the need for money or goods in short supply to help their families survive (food, tobacco, clothes, medicine or fuel). For some a love of excitement and adventure was enough reason. For others greed, self-importance or the fear of blackmail or exposure to the authorities were behind their recruitment.

Nazi wartime propaganda warning German citizens to be on the alert for spies.

Even with good motivation some potential candidates were simply not suited for the work. An overfondness for vices such as drink or sex, for example, could easily lead to indiscretions, and an inability to lie convincingly was a fatal weakness. It was also important to choose a source for a specific job and not take on someone simply because he or she was available – such people might well be double agents.

Spy cells

Once a number of sources had been recruited, the network would be split up for security reasons. Usually the agent created a series of cells, each containing between three and eight people. Only one person in

each cell would recruit a second cell, and these intermediaries between cells were always given as secure an escape route as possible to avoid their capture if a cell should be betrayed. This system ensured that counterintelligence services could capture only members of an individual cell rather than the network as a whole. Cells might be linked in a linear chain – best from a security viewpoint because each cell would be linked to, and therefore capable of giving away, only one other cell – or as a network radiating outward from the original cell, which covered larger areas more quickly.

Spotting and dealing with betrayal

Since each source presented a potential security weakness, field agents had to watch for any signs that one was compromised – either because the source might betray the organisation or because the source was under suspicion from counterintelligence. In cases like this the SOE advice was simple: If it appeared a man was a traitor, he could be frightened or paid off, but since both measures involved risks, the simplest remedy was to kill him.

To commemorate the twenty-fifth anniversary of VE (Victory in Europe) Day on 2 May 1970, General Koenig of the French Resistance shakes hands with Colonel M. J. Buckminster, head of the SOE, while undercover agent Odette Hallowes stands by.

MESSAGES AND MEETINGS

In communicating with sources, agents avoided signs of recognition unless a definite meeting had been arranged. Several agents were arrested because they smiled or waved to a source already being watched. Ideally, a meeting would fit the agent's cover story, giving it the appearance of business as usual.

Location, location, location

Wartime agents picked meeting places very carefully. Large railway stations were often closely watched, and identity papers were regularly checked there. Hotels, public meeting places, post offices and brothels were also dangerous. Waiting lines were vulnerable to informers listening in on conversations. Small hotels, restaurants, bars or cafés were better, but best of all were streets, churches, cemeteries, beaches, museums, art galleries, parks, cars and private houses or offices, all chosen to suit the cover story of the agent involved.

Sometimes both parties had identical briefcases, newspapers or even matchboxes that could be exchanged quickly before the agents each went their separate way. In picking a meeting place, the agent would check the area well beforehand to ensure that there was no cover for eavesdroppers or any other kind of counterintelligence operation.

Reading between the lines

Messages setting up a meeting gave the date and time by different methods, such as by letter and by phone. The true time would have an hour or two added, according to a prearranged formula, so if the enemy read the message, they would arrive too late to catch the agents. There would also be a prearranged danger signal that either person could give without appearing to be sending a message – such as leaving a coat unbuttoned or carrying gloves that could otherwise be kept in a pocket – to warn the other of any potential risk factors in the area.

Agents would also have a fallback arrangement to be used should anything go wrong with the original rendezvous. Each meeting place would be used once or twice only. Later meetings would use a different location at least fifteen minutes' walk away to avoid counterintelligence agents spotting patterns of behavior and becoming suspicious. In cases where the people meeting had not met previously, a third party would give a description, covering physical characteristics like height, build and apparent age. Other details would be mentioned if they were particularly distinctive. In addition, there would be an apparently casual recognition signal, like cleaning eyeglasses or using a handkerchief.

Handing over the message

The KGB was always particularly careful about meetings and message drops. In cases where information needed to be passed from one agent to another, the two agents involved would spend considerable time following one another in turn to check that neither was being tailed. Only when these checks showed that all was clear was the message passed, possibly in a false coin or a folded newspaper or as a letter.

DEAD LETTER DROPS

When handing over information directly is too risky, agents often use a 'dead letter drop', which is a prearranged site where a message can be dropped off by one agent and picked up later by another when the area is safe. The container for the message must be unobtrusive or well hidden so as not to attract the curiosity of a casual passerby – or, worse, opposition agents.

Human Agents

To alert another agent that information will be dropped off at a particular dead letter box, a signal is usually left at a *different* prearranged spot. This could be a small chalk mark on a tree trunk or on a fence post. The agent due to receive the information replies by adding a second mark or removing the first one to confirm the signal has been received.

Only after the first agent has seen this confirmation does he or she actually make the drop. Afterward the agent who picked up the material leaves another prearranged signal to confirm it has been received. The whole routine may take ten minutes or so, during which time the two agents never meet, never see each other, and are never seen together. If both agents follow separate routes through the area and change those routes from time to time, as well as appearing to show interest in several potential drop sites that are not actually used, this can be a very difficult routine for counterintelligence watchers to spot.

Spies must do their best to blend into the background and fit in with local patterns of dress and behaviour.

CAPTURE AND QUESTIONING

In spite of every careful precaution, agents may still be captured by opposition counterintelligence agents and subjected to questioning. Since spies, unlike prisoners of war, are not protected from mistreatment as stated in the Geneva Convention, they may be treated very badly by their captors. For example, they may be subjected to stress or torture to make them reveal what they know. The arrest may begin as a polite request to answer questions, followed by continued detention to prevent the possibility of warning colleagues. In other cases a raid in the small hours of the morning may try to intimidate the victim.

Interrogation techniques

Usually the questioning follows the 'bad cop, good cop' type, in which two 'cops' alternate their interviews. The 'bad cop' behaves negatively towards the subject, making blatant accusations, derogatory comments, and threats, and in general raising the subject's antipathy. This sets the stage for the 'good cop' to act in a deceptively supportive, understanding manner, and in general show sympathy for the subject, which may make the subject cooperative toward the latter.

Other techniques that add to the pressure include using strong lights and an unstable or uncomfortable chair. Skilled interrogators also use prolonged silences in an attempt to goad the prisoner to talk. They may threaten torture or execution or produce false confessions apparently written by another agent. Others will repeatedly return to earlier questioning sessions in an attempt to reveal inconsistencies or provide a reconstruction of recent events involving the agent, giving only half the story in great detail. The prisoner is then ordered to repeat what he has just been told, and the questioners will look for any detail that is added to what they said, which will confirm that the suspect really was involved.

For fear of hidden microphones, talking to fellow prisoners or to medical staff sent in to treat them is a bad idea. Agents normally try to answer questions slowly, clearly and firmly to appear convincing and to give themselves time to think. They strive to give an impression of an honest but not-too-bright citizen attempting to answer questions to the best of his or her ability.

Finally, an agent released after questioning has to be careful to act normally and in character in case surveillance continues and there is a subsequent rearrest. Often, counterintelligence agents will keep a released suspect under surveillance in the hope that he or she will lead them to other agents in their network.

TRADECRAFT
Coping with capture

Wherever possible, agents who have been captured give dead-end responses that do not give rise to further questions. Some questioners may play stupid to lower the prisoner's guard. Agents subjected to drugs try counting silently so that under the influence of the dose, they would be more likely to repeat strings of numbers than anything incriminating. Finally, an agent released after questioning has to be especially careful to act normally and in character in case surveillance continues and there is a subsequent rearrest.

Escape: the best option
The agent's best defence is to escape. The most opportune time is as soon as possible after capture while he or she is still in familiar surroundings, physically fit and in possession of clothing and equipment. Chances may arise during transfer to a more secure location. An experienced agent will use opportunities like roadblocks or refuelling stops.

Stay in control
The captured agent faces a psychological battle to control the situation. Factors like pain, fatigue, boredom, hunger, thirst, heat, cold, loneliness and fear will be used to undermine resistance. Methods like sleep deprivation, the use of truth drugs or exposure to extreme cold can dull the mind and body, weaken willpower and undermine resistance. Fatigue, boredom, and isolation will also sap resistance. This will make the prisoner more susceptible to suggestion and aggressive, threatening questioning by his captors.

Most agents are given a target amount of time to remain silent, giving their associates a chance to minimise the damage. After the time is up, they are free to give information. The danger is that the captured agent may be kept away from clocks under conditions that make time seem to pass more slowly than normal. The agent may feel the deadline has passed while still well short of it.

Examine the surroundings
One powerful incentive to remain alert and positive is to look for weaknesses in the confinement area that may allow an escape attempt. Are the walls brick, stone, blocks, timber or concrete? What about the floors and ceilings, the plumbing and the electrical fittings? What routine do the guards follow, when are meals delivered and what are the immediate surroundings that can be seen when taken to and from the cell?

A brick wall can be broken by chipping away the mortar around a single brick in an area where guards cannot easily see it – either at night, or hidden behind a bed. Mortar dust is made into a paste with water so it can fill the crack during daylight hours. Once the first brick is lifted out, adjacent bricks can be moved to make an opening big enough to climb through. Blocks can be dealt with in the same way, or where noise is not a problem, a hole can be hammered through them with a metal object. A metal bar can be used to pry timbers apart in a wooden wall, and though stone walls are more difficult, an old building may have fragile doors and windows that offer escape opportunities.

Avoid capture in the first place
Finally, the best escape method is never to be captured in the first place. Agents must maintain a high level of security and keep aware of any surveillance suggesting they are under suspicion. Tidying one's room helps reveal if police have recently searched the location. Extra precautions include hiding a dead leaf inside a keyhole or stretching single hairs across door openings, cupboards, drawers or attaché cases to reveal whether or not they have been opened by someone else.

SPYMASTERS & MASTER SPIES
Greville Wynne and Colonel Oleg Penkovsky

The need for the highest possible level of security was proved all too clearly by the case of Russian colonel Oleg Penkovsky. Following wartime service, he had been transferred to Soviet military intelligence, and by the early 1960s he was worried by his country's belligerent leadership and the prospect of nuclear war. He felt this could be avoided by contacting the West and passing information that would reveal Soviet intentions and capabilities.

His opportunity came in April 1961, when he travelled to London as head of a Soviet trade delegation. Greville Wynne, a British businessman and former intelligence agent who was organising the trade visit, went to Moscow to complete the arrangements. Penkovsky persuaded him to pass his plans to London, and when the delegation arrived, he was taken to meet British and American intelligence chiefs to check he was not a double agent with false information.

Accepting him as genuine, they then organised communications with British contacts in Moscow. These included Wynne himself, who took delivery of rolls of film and passed prearranged items of disinformation for Penkovsky to pass off as

Double agent Oleg Penkovsky, hearing himself sentenced to death in Moscow Soviet Supreme Court on 11 May 1963.

material seized while in the UK Another contact was Janet Chisholm, code-named Anne, the wife of a British embassy attaché. Penkovsky gave her a box of sweets for her children with film hidden inside it.

Discovery

All went well until he spotted someone watching one of his regular meetings with Mrs Chisholm. He noted the registration of a car making a U-turn in a nearby one-way street, carrying two men in dark overcoats in the backseat. These men, he figured, could be undercover police. Nevertheless, Penkovsky and Mrs Chisholm met again a week later and all seemed well, but the following week Penkovsky saw the same car again. Meetings were replaced by dead letter drops. One of these was a space behind a radiator in the lobby of an apartment building, and signals included a prearranged number of rings at a particular telephone number, or a black mark on a specific lamppost.

Penkovsky's last meeting with Wynne took place at a restaurant. The Russian arrived first and spotted a KGB surveillance team. He left in time to warn Wynne, who was catching a flight leaving the following afternoon. Wynne switched to an earlier flight, but three months later Penkovsky was arrested by the

The three judges before whom Wynne and Penkovsky were charged with espionage at the start of their trial in Moscow on 7 May 1963.

KGB and Wynne was seized while on a business visit to Budapest. Both were tried and convicted of espionage. Penkovsky was executed in 1963, but a year later Wynne was exchanged for a Soviet agent in Western hands.

More recently, Russian sources have claimed that the Penkovsky operation was a trap to catch Western agents, who would be used as bargaining chips to release valuable agents of their own captured by the West and to provide low-level information as the framework for positive disinformation. The full truth may never be known, but one insider's view is that Penkovsky was set up by a faction in the Kremlin who were genuinely worried about the increasing level of East–West tension. Certainly, the information he passed reassured the UK and the United States that a real missile gap still existed in their favour, and his arrest showed the Soviet leadership that the West was well aware of it. All these were vital factors in defusing the Cuban Missile Crisis in October 1962, one of the most dangerous challenges of the entire Cold War.

Tradecraft

Counterintelligence is the biggest threat spies face and they have developed a series of techniques to oppose it. These strategies are known collectively as tradecraft and are designed to protect networks against suspicion, capture and interrogation. They require extensive preplanning – everything from tighter security and careful observation to methods for detecting agent surveillance, ducking 'tails' and guarding against betrayal.

The success of any espionage operation depends on safety and security. Most important is the choice of a secure location for the network's headquarters. Safe houses, where agents under threat can find refuge, are crucial. Agents arrange meetings with their contacts in as many different places as possible. Open country is preferred, since isolation allows for quicker detection and also makes surveillance by counterintelligence more difficult. Successful agents don't leave a paper trail – they rely on memorizing plans and records.

Picking a base

Headquarters (HQ) and safe houses must be easy to get in and out of without arousing suspicion. The base should fit into a neighbourhood and not stand out. An existing business is the best cover, because it will be established in the community and give agents a plausible reason for being there. If a new business has to be set up, it should be a real one, serving the needs of the community in which it is located. A new business has to ensure agents unquestioned entrance and provide an alibi for their presence.

Defending your safe house

Safe houses are only safe if they are properly secured and defended. The choice of venue must be considered carefully. For example, a house with thick walls offers more security from eavesdroppers than a modern building

Fibre-optic cables allow agents to spy on specific locations without being observed.

The studio of Soviet spy Rudolf Ivanovich Abel, who posed as an artist in New York as his cover story for residing in the United States.

where you can hear your next-door neighbour breathe. Thick walls also offer options for concealment: Documents and even people can be hidden behind solid masonry. Street-level shops are vulnerable because police or counterespionage agents can enter easily, allowing agents little time to escape or hide. Professional offices on higher floors – doctors, lawyers, accountants – are safer, as are small inns with a clearly defined clientele. Safe houses need more than one exit, and they should lead out to different streets.

However, ensuring that agents are secure while they're in the safe house is only part of the story. Agents also have to guard against the property's being searched when no one is there. Agents must hide all incriminating materials even during temporary absences, and leave nothing behind if they are gone longer than a few days. Experienced agents know the value of planning and must avoid leaving anything incriminating in the safe house. For example, weapons are hard to destroy or dispose of at the last minute, as are coded writing, notepads, carbons (though few are still used, they still pose a danger), and even blotting paper. Burning papers might seem to be the obvious solution, but such material cannot be burned quickly. Finally, guards on the premises are essential when the safe house is in use, especially in shops or other easily accessible facilities. And finally, agents need to make sure they are not followed when leaving or entering a safe house.

Agents are not necessarily out of danger even when they are in a safe house: Complacency can be a spy's downfall. To ensure that counterintelligence agents do not spot a safe house, spies must avoid establishing set patterns of behaviour. Agents have many different tricks up their sleeves to help them confound counterintelligence agents, from the simplest things – such as changing their clothes frequently and not wearing the same clothes two days in a row – to more complex methods, like taking different routes to get to headquarters and arriving at different times each day so that no pattern about their movements can be determined. Other precautions include using prearranged signals to show whether a location is safe or in danger, such as a doormat left in a certain position or an object of a specific colour displayed casually.

ENTERING THE DANGER ZONE

Spies often need to travel across national borders, inviting numerous dangers. Some spies can travel on diplomatic or other valid passports and have acceptable reasons for travelling to a hostile country. Few try to smuggle weapons or other sensitive articles, because if they were discovered, the spies' mission would be over and their life at risk. Weapons and other sensitive material are usually brought in later.

However, some missions mean the agent must travel in secret, which complicates matters. Arriving on a hostile shore by boat means that the agent must dispose of the craft and watch out for coastal patrols. Parachuting in without a reception committee means that the agent risks injury, must dispose of the chute without being seen, and hightail it out of the immediate area as quickly as possible; the noise of the aircraft flying overhead might alert authorities on the ground. If an agent crosses a land border illegally, he or she will need a good map – and a good memory – for landmarks and border checkpoints, which are often located well behind the frontier.

Travelling through enemy territory

Moving by day arouses less suspicion and allows spies to blend in with the everyday movements of local communities. The safest time of all is during rush hour, when individuals are less conspicuous among crowds of people. As always, the key to an agent's safety and success is in the detail. First-class travel is preferable. However, buying first-class tickets may arouse suspicion at small country stations where strangers stand out and locals may remember significant details. Large junctions and city terminals may have regular control checks, so agents need to look out for alternative exits if they are fearful of being captured.

The rush-hour crowds make it easier for an agent to travel unobserved.

Blending into the surroundings

Hanging around in a town for a long time with nothing to do is especially dangerous, because the locals become suspicious and the chances are greater for agents to blow their cover. Agents should find some normal activity that blends in with the surroundings. Luggage or packages must conform to a cover story – that is, a credible explanation for being in the area in the first place. Even if an agent's journey is a fictional part of their cover story, they must know everything about the journey: the routes and times for the trains and how much the tickets cost. Their clothing must correspond to the transportation used – muddy shoes, for instance, would invalidate a story about a train trip. Agents must be familiar with local rules and regulations, especially when meeting with local officials. To avoid arousing suspicion by loitering or trying to avoid authority figures, such as police or security guards, agents should ask them innocuous questions.

Where is it safe to sleep?

The obvious hiding place would seem to be large hotels, because they are crowded and anonymous places where many people come and go, providing camouflage for the agent. However, informers and the police are aware of this, so they tend to hang around these areas, checking the registry and watching guests for any unusual behaviour. Moreover, most of the larger facilities maintain in-house detectives who often double as informers. Inns and B&Bs can be a better alternative, since they are not monitored so closely. However, they offer more of a close-knit community, where guests gossip and the owners may work with the police. An agent's best bet is therefore to work their contacts to find more secure places to live and sleep for the longer haul.

Undercover careers

In most cases, a local job is a vital part of an agent's cover story. It explains where the agent gets money to live on and why he or she is in the region. The best option is a part-time or informal job that doesn't require informing the authorities. Another option is to have an imaginary job, which involves finding a trusted employer in the network who can confirm the agent's job story if the authorities check. Other jobs call for specific technical qualifications or experience, and for these, credentials are checked and living arrangements restricted to certain areas. In all cases, the cover job should be credible; hours, pay and movements must conform to the new identity.

FICTITIOUS ALIBIS

A cover story is an agent's best insurance policy and should never be sacrificed needlessly. Therefore, agents need to stay out of trouble, since even the shrewdest cover may not survive police or counterintelligence investigations. Short-term alibis are one defence against suspicion, as long as they are plausible: Credible alibis generally do not lead to further questioning. When some implausibility is inevitable, a watertight background story will hold up under prolonged questioning.

Details help as long as they match police experience. Agents therefore need to be aware of "normal" behavior and match their own responses to this to avoid arousing suspicion. For example, people tend to remember times of trains and whether they were late or early; they would be less likely to remember when they finished a meal, though they would probably recall what they ate and whether it was good or bad.

The best alibis are those closest to the truth, with only the incriminating details changed, because they will fit in with the agent's general appearance and knowledge. The closer the cover story is to the agent's real-life experience, the easier it will be for them to remember the details and avoid arousing suspicion. After all, dates can be shifted and time stretched, but invented stories can be dangerous if they are not based on fact. At the very least, spies must have the chance to rehearse the invented details of their cover story under pressure.

In all cases, an agent's cover story should come to a dead end, leaving few loopholes for further investigation and questions, and with no direct links to other people, events or places that could prove incriminating.

WIGS AND WALKING STICKS

As part of their cover stories, agents sometimes have to assume a new identity, from superficial to profoundly intimate. In short, agents must become another person, not just look like one. They have to inhabit the character, to draw from within, where the core personality lives, so that they know where their new identity comes from, where it is headed and why, what it wants, who it is supposed to be, and what to do when it reaches the desired objective. In this way, the 'character' and the cover story will be so inseparably ingrained that it is far more likely to stand up under questioning.

Espionage often require disguise. It is not always necessary, but when it is, it can be drastic. In some cases, a simple disguise will suffice – when police have a description, or when an agent must operate in the open and can be seen easily. However, in the case of an agent sent on an assignment to his hometown where he is well known, plastic surgery may be needed to change his appearance.

As with every other aspect of the cover story, the agent's appearance must fit the assumed identity. Spies must be extremely careful when choosing the cut and style of their clothes, as well as their accessories, like the brand of cigarettes they smoke or the newspaper they carry – the smallest detail out of place can be enough to give an agent away. Should the hair be long or short, tidy or unkempt? Should the face, teeth, hands and shoes be dirty or clean and well cared for? What about the walk, handwriting, habits and associates? Absolutely everything must fit the character exactly.

Sometimes the smallest changes can have a great impact. For example, simple alterations in clothing can greatly change a person's appearance – like a switch from a smart suit to gardening clothes, or choosing stripes that run one way or the other, which can make the wearer appear shorter or taller. Moving buttons on garments can change apparent height or weight. Then there are the obvious changes: Hair colour can be changed, as can eyebrows, which can also be plucked or reshaped. Stage makeup can alter the shape of the eyes or ears, while the use of sponge pads can change the shape of the nose and cheeks. Teeth can be discoloured with iodine and the colour of eyes changed with contact lenses. Different styles of spectacles, sideburns and mustaches can also change appearance.

OPERATION SURVEILLANCE

Nevertheless, despite every effort, an agent can still arouse the suspicion of local authorities and be put under surveillance by a team of experts. They will be looking for any sign that reveals his character and habits – where he lives, what he does every day, any suspicious activities: whom he meets, where he picks up messages, if he leaves signals for others.

Spy disguises on display at the International Spy Museum in Washington, D.C.

Team cover

Surveillors are not easy to spot, because, like the agents themselves, they employ many different covers to follow their target. They will use taxis, drivers in delivery vans, bicycle messengers, shoppers, a couple strolling down the street, a woman pushing a baby carriage – anything innocuous or commonplace. They will also be experienced in handing off surveillance from one of their agents to another and can signal if the suspect has evaded his pursuers.

Common ways to avoid being spotted include not walking too closely behind the person an agent is tailing, and gauging the distance by the number of people on the street. Street lamps, cars, trucks, and even other people can serve as hiding places to prevent the suspect from detecting a tail. Crossing the street inside a crowd and walking on the other side of the road from his or her target all help to make the tail less conspicuous.

The trusty trench coat

Just as agents do their best to blend into the background, so do their tailers. Tailers tend to be short, not tall, and wear dark clothing that fits the locale and climate to avoid attracting attention. Tailers also use a range of props to help them do their job. A waterproof coat is standard equipment; so are quiet shoes. They usually carry plenty of small change, a notebook and pencil, and food. They almost always carry a newspaper or magazine: Reading gives them cover in bars, cafés and on public transit. Lighting a cigarette provides an excuse to stop and look around. A change of clothes – putting on or pulling off a coat or hat – can disguise their appearance; so can dumping a package they have carried as a prop.

On the trail

Public transit provides different challenges for tailers. They tend to sit on the same side as the person they are following. Where fares vary by distance, they will wait until the suspect buys a ticket before doing so themselves; in bars or

Tailers must use a wide variety of techniques to ensure they are not spotted by their suspect.

restaurants they will sit behind the agent in order to keep an eye on him. Ordering food that can be finished quickly and paying the bill when the order arrives allow for a quick departure. Mirrors can also be used to watch the quarry without being obvious or making eye contact with the suspect.

SPOTTING AND LOSING A TAIL
Expert sleuths are hard to detect, especially if they follow all the guidelines discussed above. They are also hard to lose, so agents must double their vigilance if they suspect they are being tailed.

Am I being followed?
Being vigilant from the outset is key. For example, a careful agent will pick the third car in line at a taxi stand – after taking a careful look at the first two and their drivers. In this way, if one of them shows up behind him during the trip, the spy will know he is probably being followed. Another common method used by spies to throw off potential tails is to give the driver a phony address before getting into the cab – for the benefit of anyone listening – and then changing the directions once inside.

It is also good practice to get out of the cab near the final destination – at a church, store, or park – rather than at the destination itself. If an agent still fears he is being followed, he can walk through the store, for example, take the elevator to an upper floor, walk around, then leave abruptly, pushing through the most crowded exit. Walking up deserted streets and changing direction often and without warning are other techniques used to ward off tails. Another option, if the tail is far enough away, is to take a second cab, repeating the same precautions.

Shaking off the enemy
Losing a tail is tricky but doable. Common techniques used by agents in the field include dashing into a subway or aboard a bus or streetcar, using lifts to move quickly through a high-rise building, or slipping into street crowds. Another tack: Pretend to be unaware and behave like everyone else.

For any of these methods to work, however, they must be carried out quite naturally, without giving the impression that the agent knows he or she is being followed. Agents who give any signal that they know they are being observed will simply make themselves more noticeable. This means that spies must be aware of, and imitate, 'normal' behaviour. For example, if they need to look around to check whether they are still being followed, they must take care never to look directly at the tail. Common techniques include stopping to tie shoelaces, looking around at a passerby, or lighting a cigarette

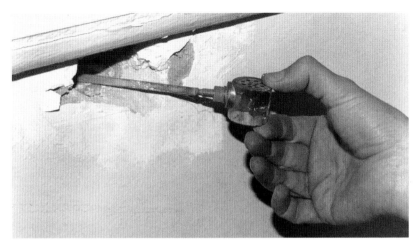

In June 1989 a microphone was found behind the plaster under a windowsill in the flat of a Russian diplomat in North London.

as a pretext to stop and take a look around. Finally, a good memory is key. If agents do spot their pursuers, they need to remember as much as possible so they can give a detailed description to other members of their network.

KEEPING THE SAFE HOUSE SAFE

In this high-tech age, computer safety is also a concern. Simply deleting incriminating files is not an option, because experts can access this information from the hard drive. Savvy spies therefore fit their computers with removable hard drives that they take out and lock up every night. That drive backs up the internal hard drive, which should be purged every four to six weeks through reformatting. Normal phones and mobile phones are easy to tap: they should never be used for sensitive information. Instead, agents keep a 'clean' telephone locked away, then plug it in and use it for security calls. Rooms should also be swept regularly to detect any bugs.

Even experienced agents are not always as careful as they should be. Oleg Penkovsky (see Chapter 3) took great care to wrap up the exposed film he was passing to the West in a matchbox, protected by layers of paper, wrapping tape, and wire. He then hung the parcel on a hook behind a radiator in the Pushkin Street apartment house, which had been agreed to as a dead letter drop. Sadly, his precautions were wasted when the KGB spotted the routine and caught on to what was being left there. Another weakness was his desire for acceptance by the West. He asked for, and was given, the rank of colonel in both the British and US armies and was photographed in the uniforms at a reception in recognition of his work. He was sentimental enough to keep copies of the photographs, which were found when the KGB searched his quarters.

TRADECRAFT
Avoiding bombs

Aftermath of a letter bomb that exploded in the offices of the London Stock Exchange on 23 August 1973.

Incoming mail also needs checking. Any packages not immediately identifiable as routine mail could contain a letter bomb. Telltale clues include a bulky package holding more than the usual two or three sheets of folded paper, or the presence of hard shapes or lumps.

A possible letter bomb can be opened relatively safely by pushing a thin piece of stiff wire through the bottom end of the envelope. First, the wire is bent into a loop at the butt end, and a piece of string at least 2.6 m (10 feet) long is tied to this loop. The package is then put on the ground and held there by a weight placed on one corner. Next, the string is pulled to rip open the bottom edge of the package from a

safe distance. It can then be picked up and examined through the bottom end to see if the contents are suspicious – most letter bombs are designed to go off if opened at the normal end of the package or when the contents are pulled out.

Car bombs are usually placed under or close to the driver's seat – triggered by the ignition circuit, by the flexing of the suspension over bumps, or externally by radio control. Normal precautions would include keeping the car in a locked garage and checking it before every journey. The agent would also need to sweep it every day to check for signs of tampering or the presence of unexplained wires, including under the bonnet and beneath the chassis.

Tools of Espionage

Every spy has to rely on his or her powers of observation and recall. From a brief glimpse of a surveillance vehicle to a quick scan of a vital document, the spy has to remember as much as possible. Sometimes the material is too detailed to reproduce accurately from memory, so spies have to find other ways of recording the information and passing it on without raising suspicions, from invisible ink to flasks with false bottoms. As technology advances, so do methods and equipment for more effective surveillance.

One of the classic coups of old-time espionage was carried out by Colonel Robert Baden-Powell, future founder of the worldwide Boy and Girl Scout movements. In the closing years of the nineteenth century, British intelligence urgently needed details of the defences of the Austro-Hungarian Empire in the highly volatile Balkans, later to prove the flash point that set off World War I.

Baden-Powell, who was based in Malta, toured the empire's Balkan provinces posing as a butterfly enthusiast, a cover that gave him a plausible reason for visiting the remote areas where the defences were located. He carried with him a sketchbook in which he recorded, in painstaking detail, the appearance of each butterfly he found. No one would associate this gentle pastime with espionage, and his sketches looked perfectly innocent when examined by the authorities. Only Baden-Powell, and later his spymasters, knew that the marks in the drawings of the wing patterns of the butterflies showed an accurate record of all the Austrian defences.

SECRET MESSAGES

Information sent by mail had to be couched in language that would fool official censors by hiding important details beneath routine text. (Sophisticated codes and ciphers would come later; see Chapter 9.)

In 1978 the KGB used an umbrella with a poison tip, much like this one, to murder Bulgarian dissident Georgi Markov.

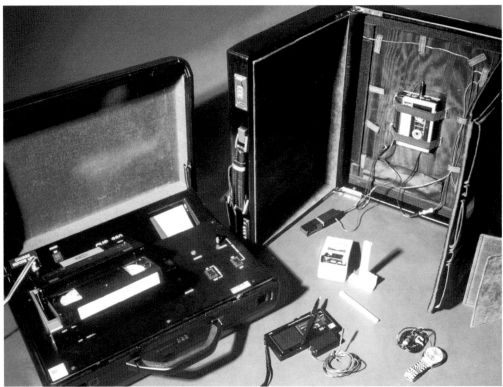

An array of spy equipment, including briefcases with a hidden video camera, and cigarette packs and wristwatches with tape recorders hidden inside.

Covering letters

A simple method involved dispatching an ordinary written communication from which the recipient could piece together a secret message by underlining every twentieth letter. In World War II captured German U-boat officers used this system to transmit data on enemy tactics in letters home to Germany discussing family matters.

Invisible ink

Other agents used secret inks to write hidden messages on the pages of seemingly routine correspondence, or even on banknotes. The secret message could then be exposed by an agent at the other end by using the correct chemical treatment. Use of these inks became problematic when counterintelligence agents began treating all mail with chemicals to reveal scattered secret texts. However, this did not lead to the demise of invisible inks; rather, it led to the development of new chemicals and treatments to stay ahead of the opposition.

Fooling the ink detectors

During World War II many invisible writing agents were known by both sides, and tests would reveal most of them. Some responded to heat, others fluoresced under a beam of ultraviolet light and others reacted to iodine fumes. The most difficult to detect, like the Pyramidon used by German agents, were also difficult to obtain. Others, like a few grains of magnesia dissolved in acetic acid, were difficult to develop once the message reached its destination – the paper had to be ironed until the heat turned it yellow and then washed in a 5 per cent solution of silver nitrate before being ironed again to show the message. One of the best combinations was a very weak solution of antipyrene – used in prescriptions for relieving headaches – that could be developed by a 10 per cent solution of ferric chloride, but which did not react to heat, iodine, or ultraviolet light.

Today's closest equivalent is the ink used in ballpoint pens. If a message is written with one of these in the normal way and the upper side of the paper is pressed against a second sheet, it will seem that the message has not been transferred because the ink dries so quickly. Yet faint traces will have been picked up on the second sheet, invisible to the naked eye. Only when the second sheet of paper is treated with the right developer will the message appear, reversed so that it has to be read with a mirror.

NEW TECHNIQUES

As invisible inks grew less popular, espionage organizations had to find new ways of hiding secret messages. For example, the KGB pioneered innovative 'packaging' to allow their agents to carry text or film past customs or police checkpoints. One technique was the use of "false bottoms," which are internal partitions put into containers such as hip flasks and cans of talcum powder, into which a message or object could be placed. Tubes of shaving cream were opened, a message or film inserted, and then the tube was resealed, burying the espionage under white cream. At first glance the container would look completely normal and would thus pass a cursory inspection. Even a roll of innocent photographs might conceal a message within the centre of the spool.

Shrinking messages

Another way of hiding a message is to shrink it so it is virtually undetectable. Microdots and high-speed burst transmissions both compress information to minimise the chances of exposure– either of the message itself or of the agent sending or receiving it.

Amazing microdots

German technicians during World War II perfected a means of photographing the full page of a sensitive document through a camera fitted with a reversed microscope lens, which shrank the image instead of magnifying it. This reduced a full page of data to a dot the size of a typewritten full stop, which could then be placed over an ordinary full stop in an entirely innocent document. Indeed, if it were hidden in a book, the recipient would have to know which page and which word identified the location of the microdot before examining it under a microscope to read the information. Anyone not in on the secret would have an enormously time-consuming task checking every punctuation mark in the book. Microdots were also hidden beneath postage stamps so that even a check of an entire text might not reveal any secret information.

High-speed transmission

High-speed radio transmissions were developed to combat the danger of direction-finding (DF) teams. This too was a German development from World War II, when Allied warships and shore stations homed in on ordinary radio transmissions from German U-boats to their headquarters. Since these messages were enciphered and then transmitted in Morse code, they took a relatively long time to send – more than enough time for direction finders to pinpoint the submarine's position and send patrols to sink it.

The Germans reduced the danger with a new transmission system, code-named *Kurier*. This sent a prerecorded message as a series of short bursts, each containing half a dozen or so letters of the message and lasting less than half a second. Each burst would switch to a different frequency, making it very difficult for the direction finders to fix the position of the submarine.

This complex system was very effective, but it had one major drawback. The equipment that received the burst signals and reassembled the message was extremely bulky, consisting of three special receivers and a display system. This was far too large for the cramped space of a submarine's radio room, so burst transmissions could be sent only in one direction. Signals from headquarters back to individual U-boats had to be sent at normal speed. The U-boat avoided sending any acknowledgement so its position was not given away. While Allied direction finders could still locate U-boats, burst transmissions made their task much harder.

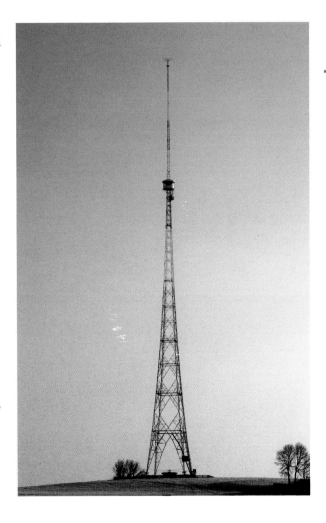

During World War II both sides tried to conceal their radio communications.

Pinpointing the transmitters

The Germans, too, used direction finding to track down agents in occupied Europe, who were transmitting to the UK. A network of fixed stations and mobile units could rapidly pin down the position of a secret transmitter to an individual building, and eventually to a single room if a long message was being sent.

Agents developed different ways of coping. Ciphers were improved to cut down message length, schedules were varied so the enemy had less warning of a transmitter being on the air and operators moved between different transmitting sites.

As the use of radios spread, transmitters became more compact and were easier to hide. Operators could move swiftly from one location to the next and stay ahead of German direction finders.

Observers were placed near broadcast sites to watch out for the arrival of mobile DF units and warn transmitters to get off the air and hide the set before it was spotted. As recording machines became more reliable, messages were speeded up. Voice or Morse code reports were prerecorded, then played on the radio at high speeds, cutting the time in which DF units could trace the signal. At the other end the high-speed message was recorded and played back at slower speeds to retrieve the content.

Technological developments

New technology made tracing more difficult. Ultra-high frequency (UHF) short-wave radio transmissions were not reflected off the Heaviside layer in the upper atmosphere. Instead, they were aimed along a line of sight to their destination so they could only be intercepted over a relatively small area, and when UHF was combined with 'burst' technology and automatic frequency changing, the transmitter was almost impossible to pinpoint.

The Office of Strategic Services (OSS) then developed another way of using these new pinpoint signals. Transmitters sent a highly directional beam vertically upwards – so that even local direction finders could not pick them up. US planes patrolled overhead at set times to receive scheduled transmissions from the ground. The transmissions would be recorded or retransmitted to an Allied base. Spoken messages were not encrypted, because distances were short and the system was secure, a huge advantage in brevity and clarity.

LISTENING IN

The most reliable means for intercepting messages is to tap into the link between sender and receiver. Usually this involves eavesdropping on the agent operating in hostile territory rather than on the actual spymasters who are located elsewhere in more secure surroundings. Telephone taps and hidden microphones have become increasingly smaller and more difficult to detect, a development which was triggered by Russia's success in bugging the US ambassador's office in Moscow in the late 1950s. The Russians gave the envoy a wooden reproduction of the Great Seal of the United States to be hung behind his desk. The bug was not discovered until 1960. When is was exposed, ambassador Lewellyn Thompson brought it back home where the then UN ambassador Adlai Stevenson used it as a prop to expose Soviet duplicity.

Miniature cameras and microphones

Development of miniature short-range transmitters has greatly increased the sophistication of miniature cameras and microphones that can be hidden in walls, ceilings and doors, or in lamps and other items of furniture to bug a room. The information these devices collect can be sent to nearby eavesdroppers who collect sensitive data or are looking for ways to blackmail foreigners into becoming their agents.

Warsaw Pact intelligence used such information to bait the so-called 'honey trap'. Agents, diplomats, and businessmen travelling officially behind the Iron Curtain would conveniently meet attractive and available women (or sometimes men). Hotel-room trysts would be photographed and recorded and the 'evidence' used to recruit the dupes for communist intelligence. Refuse and the incriminating data would be sent to wives and/or superiors. True, men of tougher mettle would tell their interrogators, 'I'll take

These miniature video cameras, also known as board cameras, include a microphone and are used for covert surveillance at home or in the workplace.

six of this and three of that and oh my wife would love four of those', but those who did not were pushed into small espionage at first and, once hooked, forced to supply heftier intelligence.

Sweeping for bugs

As hidden devices become smarter – some work on previously unused frequencies, and others are triggered only after sensors tell them someone has entered a room or after picking up the opening of a conversation – so does the sweeping equipment that agents use to find out if they're being spied upon themselves. It can now find carefully concealed microphones and cameras by sweeping the frequencies on which they operate and then monitoring their reactions.

Aiming for sound

External surveillance is another danger spies face, no matter what side they are on. Modern 'rifle' microphones – so called because of their high directional sensitivity, which demands aiming them as carefully as a gun – can pick up a conversation inside a room simply from the minute vibrations of the window panes. Other optical devices, using lasers or microwaves, can focus on objects within the room and, for example, make pictures hanging on a wall visible outside. In one celebrated demonstration, a manufacturer of this type of commercially available equipment was able to pick up a conversation conducted inside a car, with all the windows closed and parked in the middle of an open field, by focusing on the vibrations of the driver's sun visor.

SEEING IN THE DARK

Spy cameras, beloved by fictional agents, needed a lot of light to produce clear images, meaning the spy had to switch on office lights or use a flashgun to photograph documents or records – and thus make himself vulnerable to early detection. Fortunately for the spy, this is no longer the case. New technology enables spies to see in the dark – from sophisticated cameras to satellite technology.

Infrared cameras

Today's infrared cameras can operate in very low levels of ambient light, and digital cameras can not only produce pictures under totally unpromising conditions, but the electronic information contained in those pictures can be sent anywhere in the world over the Internet or as e-mail attachments. Specialised digital cameras can be used for surveillance by leaving them at a sensitive location disguised as, or hidden in, part of the background scenery – a stone, a pile of logs or a box – where they can take and transmit pictures when triggered by a specific instruction or a signal from a movement detector.

Night-vision systems

Night-vision systems make it possible to watch out for people or information, even in absolute darkness. Thermal imagers use a beam of infrared light, invisible to the naked eye, to illuminate objects and people in darkness, obscured by mist, driving snow, cloud or smoke. Unfortunately, the light this device emits can be picked up on another infrared device, but this can be avoided by using a passive image intensifier. This produces images in dark conditions by taking very low levels of ambient light (moonlight,

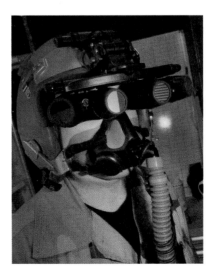

Experimental night-vision goggles enable humans to see in the dark.

starlight or diffused light from artificial sources) and converting the light signals into electrons, amplifying them, and turning the resulting signal back into light. This gives a greenish image of the scene at the screen or eyepiece of the intensifier, which would otherwise be quite invisible to the observer.

Satellite tracking

Satellite-based navigation tools – known as Global Positioning System (GPS) – show the precise location of individuals and the vehicles they are using, be they cars, aeorplanes or sailing boats. Four satellites monitor movements and when a receiver picks up their signals, it can calculate the target's exact position – latitude, longitude and altitude. GPS tracking devices, moreover, allow monitoring of cars and persons in real time, provided a tracker is planted on a suspected agent or his vehicle. The system triggers an alarm as soon as the suspect leaves a preset area.

The system can be combined with mobile communications to link surveillance team members tracking a suspect. Tracking devices can be fitted to a target vehicle in minutes. Powered by the car's battery, it can broadcast its position to tracking vehicles anywhere in the world. If time is short, trackers can be fixed to the target vehicle using their own strong magnets, though in this case its life is limited by the strength of its internal batteries.

Europe's Galileo GPS satellite network, illustrated below, is due to be operational in 2008. Its applications will include car, train, and aircraft guidance, road use, and rescue services.

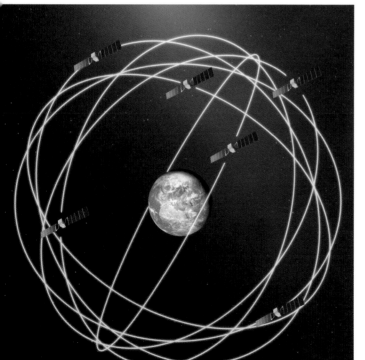

WEAPONS OF THE ASSASSIN

Agents in the field face constant pursuit from counterintelligence agents eager to track their movements, find their sources and haul them in for questioning. However, field agents also have a growing arsenal of methods to help them avoid capture, keep their secrets or hide their identities.

At times, however, agents need to call on more proactive ways of dealing with the opposition. These methods can sometimes include violence – either for self-protection or on orders to take out opponents or double agents.

Murder by poison

The most notorious case of murder by poison involved Bulgarian dissident Georgi Markov. While waiting for a bus on London's Waterloo Bridge on 7 September 1978, he was jabbed by the tip of a furled umbrella carried by a passerby (a KGB operative). The resulting puncture wound seemed trivial but soon became inflamed. Markov suffered a violent fever, convulsions and delirium and died four days later.

A postmortem revealed that the wound contained a tiny spherical pellet that had probably been fired by a gas-operated gun concealed within the furled umbrella. Holes in the pellet contained poison that was identified as ricin. He was not the first Bulgarian dissident attacked: a year earlier in Paris, Vladimir Kostov had been shot in the back with a similar device. The pellet, however, missed the main blood vessels and he survived. Police found the incriminating poisoned pellet in his tissues.

Miniature guns

Other KGB weapons used for assassinations included miniature gas-operated guns disguised as ballpoint pens or cigarette packages. During World War II the British Special Operations Executive (SOE) developed a range of single-

During World War II the KGB used pen guns to carry out assassinations. Eastern Europe has recently introduced the mobile phone gun.

shot assassination weapons, including the Welrod silenced handgun, small enough to be easily hidden, and the Welpipe single-shot weapon, which could be concealed in a tobacco pipe, cigarette, or fountain pen. The closest present-day equivalent is the mobile phone gun, developed in Eastern Europe. The casing splits into two parts with room for four 0.22 shells. The gun is cocked by a button at the base, and each round is fired by pressing a button on the dialing keypad.

Baubles or blades?

The hijackers in the 9/11 conspiracy were able to take over airliners armed with nothing more than knives, showing that the most basic weapons can sometimes be the most deadly. Today knives can be hidden in all sorts of outwardly innocent items. Blades can be folded out of keys, key-ring fobs, belt buckles, necklace pendants and even crucifixes. Others have been hidden in coins, pens, credit cards, cigarette lighters, money clips, combs, hairbrushes or lipsticks. These tiny knives, with blades less than an inch long, are primarily intended as escape tools, to cut bonds or loosen doors or windows. But they can also be used as a weapon in extremely close quarters, used to threaten the eyes or throat of a hostage or captor.

Knife blades made of plastic or ceramic materials do not show up on X-rays and have been hidden in books, cans of hairspray or shaving cream, or inside a pager holder. Umbrellas and walking sticks have been modified to conceal swords, and packs of playing cards have been made with a concealed razor-sharp edge on each card, for throwing at a target.

This blade, hidden in the heel of a shoe, is intended primarily as an escape tool but can also be used as a weapon.

TRADECRAFT
Breaking and entering

Spies often have to obtain information locked in a house or office, meaning they have to break in.

Scaling a building

Light assault ladders, easy to carry at night, are used to gain access to an upstairs window. Some are much wider than normal, allowing one agent to open the window while another enters the building. Or they can rappel down from the roof on ropes. Agents may be able to reach the roof of the building relatively easily and, once there, are less visible than at ground level. If they *have* to enter from ground level, they can use a set of four Spiderman suction pads: computer-controlled vacuum pads powered from a compressed air supply carried on the climber's back. One pad at a time is removed from the wall and shifted to a new position before suction is applied. They can grip firmly enough to support a one-tonne load on almost any surface, including smooth glass or metal.

Breaking in through doors and windows

Opening doors and windows quickly can be done using a wide choice of tools. These include hooked bars to shatter toughened glass and then remove the remains, and rams and rippers to force open different types of doors. Door spreaders can lift doors off their hinges, and special types of disc cutters can cut through metal bars. Special cartridges fired from Magnum shotguns can shatter armoured glass and blow off door hinges, and others can blow holes in doors and fill the room on the inside with an irritant gas to incapacitate anyone within.

Getting through walls

Even thick walls present no obstacle with the right tools. A portable thermal lance is powerful enough to cut through hardened steel. A special wall-breaching cannon has been developed for hostage-rescue situations when use of explosives would endanger

Spies should practise their lock-picking skills.

those held inside. The gun launches a water-filled plastic container from a smooth-bore barrel using compressed air. This has enough energy to blast a hole large enough to allow entry through a wall without harming the contents of the room beyond.

Picking locks

Lock-picking tools enable agents to gain entry through locked doors with minimum noise or disturbance. These tools consist of different shapes of picks to suit different locks, together with a range of tension bars to apply pressure to the pins inside the lock, exactly like a key. Raking involves inserting the pick right through to the rear of the lock and using a tension bar to apply enough force to push up each of the lock pins in sequence as the pick is pulled out. The tension bar is also used to twist the barrel of the lock far enough in the unlocking direction to keep the pins in position as the pick is pulled out.

Locks that do not respond to raking need to be picked – raising each pin in sequence one at a time. This calls for more skill and takes more time but may be the only way of opening the lock without leaving obvious signs. Other methods, like drilling through the lock or forcing it, may save time but leave obvious clues that security has been breached.

Double Agents

Almost every aspect of espionage is based on deceit. Survival in a hostile environment requires a completely bogus identity— false names, false papers and a false life story. This makes espionage a complex business, even with absolute loyalty and commitment. But spymasters are always aware that even their best spies may be double agents. For all kinds of reasons they may switch loyalties to work for the opposition. If there is any chance of this, their information will be suspect. Is it genuine, or is the opposition distorting the truth?

This true-or-false riddle is a simplification. Your agent may be completely loyal, but the enemy may still be feeding him or her false information. If any agents are betrayed, the opposition may simply respond by arresting or killing them. Or they may turn them, by direct or indirect threats, into members of their own team. Or they may manage to control the supply of information by passing off their own agents as reliable contacts. In that case, loyal agents will be relaying false and misleading material in perfectly good faith, convinced it represents the truth.

This is a fatal weakness if the information is assumed to be true. If information is discovered or even suspected to have been deliberately planted (known in the trade as 'disinformation'), the initiative can be taken back. A spymaster can then mislead the enemy into believing that their attempts to trick him or her have been successful. This means the situation can develop into bluff and counterbluff to the point where each side is trying to work out what the other side knows and truth and falsehood become entirely obscured.

Where only a single channel of information exists, deciding whether it is true or false is almost impossible. The only successful counter is to build up intelligence from as many different sources as possible. Where they all tend to confirm the same picture, then chances are this is the truth. A single discrepancy in one particular source is probably deliberate disinformation.

KGB mole Harold 'Kim' Philby, a member of the Cambridge Circus, betrayed Western agents sent into Albania, leading to their arrest, torture and execution.

ASSESSING INFORMATION

In wartime, questions of double agents and disinformation become especially difficult. Allied spymasters lacked multiple spy networks in the hostile and tightly controlled worlds of Nazi-occupied Europe, so they had to be especially careful in assessing apparently vital information. But Hitler's Reich had its weaknesses too. With so many men serving in its armed forces, its economy depended on huge numbers of workers from the defeated countries being put to work inside Germany.

The Germans also failed to control many other sources of information. The hugely valuable Enigma decrypts allowed the Allies to listen in on the Germans' own signals and therefore provided access to genuine information, a yardstick against which information from individual agents could be measured. In other cases, important information might be confirmed as genuine by a fragment of intelligence so completely unrelated to the main sources of information that even the most clever deception plan would hardly have thought to take it into account.

Uncovering Hitler's Revenge Weapons

During World War II the Allies made huge efforts to discover the secrets of Hitler's so-called 'Revenge Weapons'. These were principally the V1 flying bomb and the V2 ballistic missile. Fragments of intelligence pointed to a highly secret research centre at Peenemunde on the Baltic Sea coast. Though photoreconnaissance aircraft watched the area and attempts were made to place agents among the workers at the site, there was always the possibility that Peenemunde might be an elaborate "plant" to distract the Allies from looking for the genuine facility somewhere else.

Two unrelated pieces of information revealed it as a genuine target. Dr R. V. Jones, wartime head of Air Ministry

The Allies used photoreconnaissance aircraft in an attempt to discover the secrets of Hitler's 'Revenge Weapons', believed to be located at Peermunde, the German research station on the coast of the Baltic Sea.

ESPIONAGE

Intelligence, was given an intercepted enemy signal showing priorities for allocations of increasingly scarce fuel reserves in wartime Germany. Second on the list was Peenemunde, and it seemed to Jones that the Germans would never cover their tracks to this extent merely to protect a deception. He also knew that one of the only German units able to track rockets in flight was the Air Signals Experimental Regiment. If Peenemunde was genuine, this unit would have to turn up there sooner or later.

When an Enigma signal was decoded reporting the unit as moving to Peenemunde, this confirmed the site as genuine. Photographs taken by high-flying aircraft showing rocketlike objects on railroad wagons close to the site showed the real thing rather than a deceptive mock-up. Later, when V1 flying bombs were launched on test flights out over the Baltic, the British were able to intercept and decode the unit's reports of the ranges and speeds of each test, giving much-needed data on how the flying bombs could be attacked once they were launched against London.

DEADLY MISTAKES
In some cases, false information has proved extremely damaging. The capture of a radio transmitter by the Germans, and missed security checks from an enemy interception, prove how important it is to follow the rules of espionage.

Captured radio transmitter
The German Abwehr counterintelligence service arrested an agent named Hubert Lauwers, who had been sent into occupied Holland to organise supplies and weapons for the Dutch Resistance. Since he carried his own radio transmitter, this gave the Germans the chance of forcing Lauwers to send back messages to the SOE in London to organise further drops, resulting in the capture of more agents and the crippling of the Allied spy network in the Netherlands.

All espionage services have to be aware that their agents may be captured and turned by the enemy at any time. If the Abwehr simply used their own radio operator to send signals back to London on the captured set, a trained listener would know that someone else was sending the message. Each operator had an individual rhythm of sending Morse code messages, as impossible to fake as fingerprints. But what if agents were forced to send German signals under threats or torture?

The answer was a set of security checks, deliberate mistakes in a coded message that would confirm all was well. If an agent was sending a message under duress, the text would be perfectly correct and this would act as an alarm call that all was *not* well. Lauwers carefully left out these mistakes in all his messages to stop London from sending more agents and supplies. Yet the communications continued. The drops went ahead and were intercepted by the Germans, together with more than fifty agents, most of whom were shot as spies. Desperate to raise the alarm, Lauwers even added the letters 'cau' and 'ght' at the start and end of signals to confirm his fate, but this too went unnoticed in London.

The Germans continued to wreck the Allied espionage and sabotage effort in Holland for almost a year. The British realised the truth only after a series of warning signs. The first was the suspiciously high rate of lost flights over occupied Holland. Another was the absence of wrongly coded and therefore unreadable messages received from agents in Holland. Spies, sending signals quickly before the German radio direction-finding vans pinpointed their location, often made coding mistakes so a signal appeared as gibberish when it reached London. Free of this pressure while working under German control, all the Dutch messages were perfectly readable from the beginning.

Why was the absence of security checks not spotted? Was it incompetence or a deliberate policy to sacrifice agents' lives to plant false information on the Germans? The truth may lie somewhere in between. It was surprisingly common for operators, who were sending messages quickly to avoid discovery, to forget security checks. Since this happened quite often, it did not raise a red flag.

Missed security checks

In another case a British operator suspected that a signal had a different rhythm from that of the genuine agent. Surmising that it was sent by a German, he added the letters 'HH' (for 'Heil Hitler'), often used as a sign-off code by German signalers. He received 'HH' as an automatic response, confirming his suspicions. His report was ignored, and it was not until two of the captured agents escaped from German cells while waiting for execution and made their way back to London that the truth was revealed.

DOUBLE-CROSSING THE ABWEHR

The German success was soon to be eclipsed by the efforts of the British Twenty Committee ('Twenty' stood for 'XX' or 'double cross'). This involved the rounding up of every German agent sent into Britain during the war. Some were turned – to communicate with the German authorities under British control – and others were imprisoned or executed, to be replaced by fictitious, locally recruited agents who relayed false information back to Berlin.

Misleading the enemy

The stakes were extremely high. The intention was to deceive the enemy over the timing and location of the Allied invasion in the summer of 1944. There were only two logical possibilities – the Pas de Calais on the narrowest part of the Channel opposite Dover, or the more distant crossing, to the coast of Normandy, where the landings actually took place. Convincing the Germans the objective was the Pas de Calais would keep massive enemy reserves away from Normandy. There was no room for error. If the deception was revealed, these reserves would be moved to Normandy as the only other possible invasion point.

The Allies had two major advantages. Britain was an island and did not have large numbers of foreign workers from occupied countries. With no reservoir of potential agents within the country, the only agents the Germans could send into Britain were either Irish, since Eire was neutral, or disaffected Britons who had moved to Germany before the war. Both groups would speak English well enough to merge safely into the background and eventually send back information.

Rounding up German agents

In practice they were quickly rounded up. Wartime Britain was full of restrictions, of which even recent inhabitants were not aware. Lone travellers in coastal areas, where many agents landed by U-boat, came under greatest suspicion. Even if they reached towns or villages, they would still stand out among a population conditioned to the threat of invasion and the danger of German spies.

Agents are always instructed to report on papers, passes and security checks so that follow-up agents can be supplied with more convincing forgeries. The British therefore ensured that their double agents sent back disinformation. In all, the Germans sent in more than thirty agents—half a dozen through neutral Ireland and the rest by submarine and parachute—and all were safely locked up.

British World War II posters warned the public about the possibility of German spies being in the UK.

THE INVASION THAT NEVER CAME

As the deception intensified, information that was passed to the Germans by their 'agents' showed a huge buildup of Allied troops in southeast England (close to the Pas de Calais), but nothing of the genuine buildup in the southwest (close to Normandy). In case of German reconnaissance flights, huge quantities of dummy tanks, planes and even landing craft were placed all over the southeast in Kent and parts of Essex. All the coded signals traffic associated with the invasion buildup was sent by landline to a transmitter in the southeast – the Germans could not read the signals but knew the location of the transmitter and guessed it was close to the centre of the fictitious preinvasion buildup.

Double-agent Garbo
One of the most important and dedicated double agents of World War II was a Spaniard named Juan Pujol Garcia, who was originally turned down by British intelligence. Undeterred, he approached the Abwehr, where he was taken on. He then returned to Britain and volunteered his services as a ready-made double agent. This time he was accepted, and under the code names of 'Garbo' for the British and 'Cato' or 'Arabel' for the Germans, he played a crucial role in convincing the Germans that the invasion, when it finally came in Normandy, was merely a feint to persuade them to move heavy reinforcements from the Pas de Calais. The German reserves therefore remained at the Pas de Calais, waiting for a follow-up attack that never came. By the time the Germans realised they had been duped, the landings had been successfully completed.

POSTWAR DOUBLE AGENTS
Since 1945 the cold war in Europe provided more fertile ground for double agents. As Germany lay divided into zones on opposite sides of the Iron Curtain, it was relatively easy for Soviet-backed intelligence services to pass agents across the interzone border posing as refugees. Their experiences in the East made them tempting targets for Western intelligence, and once recruited, they could then pass disinformation from East to West but genuine intelligence back to the East.

In some cases, agents found high-level work. The husband-and-wife team of Gunther and Christl Guillaume were recruited by the East German espionage service by using Gunther's past membership in a Nazi Party organisation as a reason for blackmail. When they arrived in the West, they joined the Social Democratic Party and Christl secured work as a secretary in the office of German chancellor Willi Brandt. Gunther later joined her in the chancellor's office, where he became a friend and trusted colleague of Brandt. For years the couple sent the most sensitive and secret information back to the East, until they were unmasked in 1974. So fierce was the resulting scandal that it wrecked the political career of the previously popular and successful chancellor.

DOUBLE AGENTS, MOLES AND SLEEPERS

For the genuine spy sent into opposition territory, the greatest danger remains the point at which he or she has to recruit local subagents to supply the information they need to relay back to their own controllers. In some cases these people may be double agents to begin with – having reported the initial approach by the spy, they may then have been ordered to cooperate and feed them with false information. In other cases they may be slipshod, careless and overconfident and become noticed by the counterintelligence teams on their own side. Careful surveillance could easily result in the original agent being captured and then forced into collaboration, however strong their loyalty to their own side and however reluctant their cooperation.

In many ways, double agents can be confused with 'moles' or 'sleepers'. The end results may be similar, since these agents are encouraged to find work that allows them both to uncover information and frustrate the espionage activities of those countries' intelligence services. Moles, such as Kim Philby and Anthony Blunt, usually work for a long period of time in the institutions of their native country for the enemy that recruited them. Sleepers are similar – and often the terms are virtually interchangeable – but they are best described as deep-penetration agents who are usually natives of the country employing them, have emigrated to live in the target country, are fully absorbed in the language and culture and are activated by their spymaster only when the right opportunity arises. Both moles and sleepers often earn the trust and even the loyalty of those who accept them at face value (see Chapter 7).

In general, a double agent is one that for different reasons changes loyalty from the country that originally employed them as an agent to the opposition they originally worked against. Their value to the opposition – and the

Life magazine cover of 23 March 1959, showing the various identity papers of a Soviet agent.

danger to their original service – stems from this switch in loyalties, yet the fact that they have changed sides leaves them vulnerable to doubts from both their original backers and their new masters. Even in the relatively few cases where they later become disillusioned or disappointed and switch back to their first service as treble or even multiple agents, these divided allegiances invariably reduce the value of the information they produce, however sensitive and valuable it may appear to be.

In the final analysis, espionage is all about information, and information can sometimes be used to reveal a double agent with a high degree of reliability. In cases where an agent is suspected of relaying false information for the opposition, counterintelligence experts with other sources of information are often able to prime them with false intelligence. Because this information is given only to the suspect, its appearance through their other sources in the opposition is proof that their disinformation was passed on, and the compromised agent can then be used as a regular disinformation channel to confuse and frustrate the opposition espionage teams.

Gunter Guillaume, former consultant to former German chancellor Willy Brandt, and his wife Christel at their trial before the Supreme Court on 28 June 1975. Guillaume was accused of spying for the German Democratic Republic, his wife of complicity.

ESPIONAGE IN ACTION
Masters of Defection

Soviet agents working in the United States were equally successful at recruiting sympathisers to remain undercover, until they progressed to sensitive enough positions to be activated into working agents. In many cases, though, their loyalty to communism proved more vulnerable to the reality of what the Soviets were doing, and several confessed to the authorities, leading to the arrest of many fellow agents. One of the first was an academic named Elizabeth Bentley, who had seen fascism firsthand when studying in prewar Italy and who joined the American Communist Party at age 27 in 1935. She later worked for the Soviets as an agent in the United States during the 1930s and 1940s.

This gave her the identities and backgrounds of many other agents, and when she began a relationship with Peter Heller, rumored to be working for the FBI, the Russians became exceedingly worried. Philby (see page 85) reported that Bentley was working with the FBI, and they considered an assassination attempt. In the end they were forced back into damage limitation, including the rescue of Donald Maclean of the Cambridge Circus, who they feared would be implicated by her revelations.

Whittaker Chambers and Alger Hiss

Whittaker Chambers was a journalist who joined the Communist Party ten years before Elizabeth Bentley, at age 24. From 1932 he worked as a Soviet courier but changed sides in 1938, when he reported all he knew to the FBI, leading to the uncovering of a major Soviet agent – a State Department lawyer named Alger Hiss. Hiss denied any involvement with the Russians but was tried and jailed for perjury in 1950. One of the crucial pieces of evidence was a typewriter used by Hiss's wife to copy secret documents ten years earlier. The FBI traced the machine through a series of later owners, and slight misplacements of individual letters proved it had been used to copy the information.

In fact, the authorities knew of his guilt before Chambers confessed. Not only had the breaking of the KGB codes in the Venona operation (see pages 144–45) implicated him, but he was also betrayed by the first of an increasingly valuable source of inside information – a Soviet defector. Cipher expert Igor Gouzenko, working at the Russian embassy in Ottawa, crossed over to the West in September 1945. The information he brought provided the first proof of Soviet activities to subvert the interests of their allies.

Moles and double agents

The British double agent George Blake had been working for MI6 during the 1950s, having been recruited by the KGB in 1948. While working in Berlin, he learned of the Anglo-American Operation Gold, which involved the digging of a tunnel under the East–West border in the city to eavesdrop on Russian communications (see page 169). He alerted his Soviet masters to this plan. Eventually his activities were revealed by the defector Michal Goloniewski, who worked as a CIA double agent while he was a member of Polish Intelligence (UB) and who finally defected in 1961. Blake was recalled, charged and sentenced to prison.

One of the most spectacular defectors was Oleg Gordievsky, appointed head of the KGB's London station in 1984. He was already working as a double agent for the West but was recalled to Moscow in 1985, where he was warned he was about to be arrested. His betrayal came from another American double agent, Aldrich Ames (see pages 164 and 168), who exposed several US and British spies to his Soviet masters while working for the CIA, until finally arrested in 1994. British intelligence agents managed to smuggle Gordievsky out of Moscow to the West for a series of detailed debriefings. Ironically, when the Americans questioned him, much of the work was done by a prominent member of the CIA's counterintelligence team – the same Aldrich Ames!

SPYMASTERS & MASTER SPIES
The Cambridge Circus

Moles and sleepers present different problems. Some individuals sympathise so strongly with the political systems of other countries that they are willing to work on their behalf against the nation of their birth, and the degree to which they blend in with that society makes them very valuable to their new employers. For the West, it was their fellow citizens with strong Marxist sympathies who proved prime recruitment targets for the espionage organisations of the Soviet Union and its satellites. Often they were able to pass on information from their existing careers – like the scientists responsible for developing the atomic and hydrogen bombs during the 1940s and 1950s.

Others were recruited before their careers had placed them where they could have direct access to such sensitive information, but they were nurtured by their spymasters to progress into positions of power as an investment for the future. These were the 'moles' and 'sleepers' who would eventually betray so much information, and so many agents, to the Russian opposition services, causing stupendous damage to Britain and its Allies.

The Apostles Club
Perhaps the keenest moles were those Cambridge undergraduates, mainly from King's and Trinity Colleges, who were also members of the secretive Apostles Club during the 1930s. Most were closet Communists, and the man believed to have established the

Anthony Blunt, the longest-serving member of the Cambridge Circus, passed details to his Russian masters while working for MI6 during World War II.

Soviet recruitment drive, an Austrian named Arnold Deutsch, was careful to encourage his targets to adopt outwardly right-wing causes as part of their protective camouflage.

The longest-serving member of the so-called Cambridge Circus, Anthony Blunt, found a job working for British military intelligence (MI6) during the war. He passed details to his Russian masters of the governments-in-exile of Eastern European countries like Czechoslovakia and Poland, which had been set up in wartime London. This greatly helped Stalin absorb them into his satellite empire after hostilities were over.

Because Blunt had been careful covering his tracks, and because of his postwar work as art adviser to the queen, he remained free of suspicion. His fellow members were less fortunate. Kim Philby pretended to be right wing and managed to work as a reporter covering the Spanish Civil War from the anti-Communist side, earning him a medal from General Franco and a job in MI6 after the outbreak of war. His career flourished, and from 1944 he was given the job of countering Soviet espionage efforts in Britain. He was later appointed to Washington to liaise between MI6 and the CIA and managed to betray Western agents sent into Albania who were arrested, tortured and executed.

The third and fourth members of the Circus, Donald Maclean and Guy Burgess, proved the weakest links. Maclean worked for the Foreign Office in the United States and passed valuable information to the Russians. When the Americans partially decrypted the Venona messages (see pages 144–45), the evidence pointed to Maclean as the only person with access to all the leaked data. In addition, it seemed likely that the revelations of Elizabeth Bentley (see page 83) would also implicate him.

Escape

Fortunately for the Russians, Philby was told of the investigation. He alerted them to the danger, and on 25 May 1951, Maclean and the notoriously indiscreet Guy Burgess left Britain on a ferry to mainland Europe and lifelong refuge in Russia. Philby and Blunt were able to cover their tracks by destroying incriminating papers, and Philby worked for the KGB for another four years. Mounting suspicion and direct pressure from the CIA led to his

Donald Maclean escaped to Russia with Guy Burgess in May 1951 after they were exposed as spies.

sacking, though a lack of direct evidence kept him from arrest. He moved to Beirut and continued working as a journalist until he finally left for Russia in January 1963.

The fifth member of the Circus, Donald Cairncross, was recruited at Cambridge in 1933 by James Klugmann, a British Communist Party member, and was run by Anatoli Gorski, the same KGB controller who ran the other members of the Cambridge Circus. His work as a Treasury civil servant lacked direct access to sensitive information, but after the war began, he worked on the Enigma program at Bletchley Park, dealing with decrypted German signals. He passed information to his Russian masters for four years. His guilt was finally revealed after Philby's defection but was only made public after the opening of KGB files in the 1990s. As an end note, a London *Daily Telegraph* report in September 2005 claimed that the Apostles Club was still operating in Cambridge as secretively as ever.

Spy vs Saboteur

In the past, spies searched mainly for information. They were protected by anonymity and unobtrusiveness, in the case of the lone agent, or by their fame, in the case of diplomatic spies who moved in exalted circles. But during the bitter years of the German occupation of Europe in World War II, a more powerful ingredient was added to the espionage mixture with dramatically different priorities – the saboteur was recruited to destroy enemy assets.

From the summer of 1940, when the capitulation of France left the United Kingdom as Hitler's only remaining adversary, Prime Minister Winston Churchill fretted about Britain's relative inability to hit back at an enemy that dominated the Continental mainland. The remedy for this problem proved to be a new secret organisation called the Special Operations Executive, or SOE. Realising that German victories over France, Scandinavia and the Low Countries would result in the Nazis pillaging all the resources of their subject peoples in order to grow stronger and more powerful, Churchill decided on a major sabotage campaign to derail this process.

The mission of the SOE, also known as 'Churchill's Secret Army', was to encourage and facilitate espionage and sabotage behind enemy lines and to serve as the core of a resistance movement in Britain itself in the possible event of an Axis invasion. SOE agents were therefore sent into Nazi-occupied countries and told to 'set Europe ablaze'.

The task of the SOE was made easier by the fact that Germany faced the huge task of controlling such a large subject population that was growing angrier and more impatient from shortages, rationing and conscription to German industries. In this atmosphere even occasional acts of sabotage were enough to worry the occupiers.

For instance, cutting a telephone cable forced the Germans to send out repair parties and caused delay to operational orders. Blowing up factories

Woman running from a burning building after a fire was started by a Nazi saboteur during World War II.

producing German weapons and assassinating German sentries, however, often triggered bloodthirsty reprisals, such as the execution of hostages. This simply stiffened resistance further.

The actions and presence of the SOE also inspired the native populations of Nazi-occupied countries to fight back against the Germans, as well as aiding the SOE to recruit subagents willing to inform on their occupiers.

SABOTAGING THE SABOTEURS

These acts of sabotage and their consequential reprisals tended to take place with little or no warning and were counter to the organisation of conventional espionage. Spies seeking information rather than opportunities

The SOE worked closely with the French Resistance on acts of sabotage against the Nazi occupiers.

for sabotage needed peace and quiet, duping the authorities into complacency. In contrast, SOE's aim was to create turbulent conditions, and it often backed antiestablishment organisations such as the Communists in several countries. MI6, responsible for maintaining British espionage networks in Occupied Europe, saw SOE as bungling amateurs, stirring up the enemy with acts of sabotage of doubtful value. All too often they felt SOE compromised MI6's more patient campaigns in the quest for genuinely important information.

Unfortunately, SOE depended on MI6 for many essential services, and there was real suspicion that deliberate attempts were made to sabotage the saboteurs. For example, MI6 was responsible for producing the forged papers necessary for any agent to move around under the tightly controlled occupied territories. Several SOE agents claimed to have been arrested and interrogated because their papers were not up to standard. Despite MI6 denials, SOE decided to make their own false documents, which they claimed solved the problem. Accusations that SOE agents or operations were deliberately betrayed to the enemy to keep things quiet for the 'real' espionage networks were made with genuine bitterness but produced consistent denials both during and after the war.

SLEEPER AGENTS

Perhaps the diametric opposite to the spy-as-saboteur role of SOE was the role adopted by the Soviet military intelligence organisation, GRU, and later by the KGB and its satellite services. This was the idea of the spy as 'sleeper', an agent who would be placed in an overseas posting as a long-term investment so that they never came under suspicion and could gain access to places and people impenetrable to conventional 'outsider' agents.

The techniques for placing a sleeper, or putting him or her 'to bed', as espionage slang described it, usually began with the birth certificate of someone in the target country who had died in infancy or childhood. This could be used to apply for a genuine passport, which would be developed into a full-scale profile of a person who grew up in that area.

Putting a sleeper to bed

This was a long and thorough process. Soviet agents in the target country would check out schools in the area of the sleeper's supposed childhood, finding out the names of local characters and details of local events. Papers would be professionally forged, giving details of military service, together with letters and photographs from family and girlfriends. The sleeper would be taught a trade to match his or her cover story and would then go to another part of the Western world with the same language and a similar culture to help perfect the act. Finally they would become established or, in terms of the carefully built-up false identity, reestablished in the selected target country.

Sleepers sometimes spent years living within their host country without ever attracting the attention of the authorities. They spoke the language fluently, understood the customs and culture and had the papers and background story of a native. In such a position they were often able to build careers that took them to positions of power and influence. There they might have direct access to sensitive information and, in some cases, could even control or influence decisions and policies within the host country in favour of the country that had placed them there.

Sleepers betrayed

The main weakness of sleepers, however convincing their cover, has been their vulnerability to the actions of others. They have been revealed by the mistakes or indiscretions of their controllers or through the defection of those who knew their names and identities. One classic example was the Soviet master spy Colonel Rudolf Abel, who infiltrated the United States via Canada in 1948. His controllers had built on his skill as an artist and photographer to establish him with a thriving business in Brooklyn under the name of Emil Golfus. There he ran a large and successful network of Russian agents and spied on the UN headquarters in Manhattan.

BELOW LEFT Soviet spy Rudolf Abel was exchanged for Francis Gary Powers, whose U-2 plane had been shot down over the USSR.

BELOW RIGHT Superintendent Harry McMullen managed the apartment in which Rudolf Abel lived.

ESPIONAGE IN ACTION
America and Iran

Even apparently well-timed acts can have long-term repercussions. In 1953 the prime minister of Iran, Mohammad Mossadegh, threatened Western oil supplies in his push for a more independent foreign policy. The West was also worried about Iran's proximity to the USSR, when allegations that Mossadegh was a Communist led to suspicions that Iran was in danger of falling under the influence of the Soviet Union. In contrast, a pro-United States Iran under the shah would give America a strategic advantage in the Cold War, especially since Turkey, which also bordered the USSR, was already part of the NATO alliance. In a covert operation known as Operation Ajax, agents from the United States and Great Britain engineered the overthrow of Mossadegh, handing increased power to the shah, who suppressed internal dissent through his Savak secret police.

Demonstrators burn an American flag during a demonstration in front of the US embassy in Tehran, December 1979.

Short-term gain, long-term problems
In the short term, Western oil supplies were protected and the United States gained another ally in the Cold War. However, the long-term consequences were far less positive. Public opinion in Iran turned against the monarchy, culminating in the overthrow of the shah by the Islamic fundamentalist regime of the late Ayatollah Khomeini in 1979. American involvement with the shah's rule resulted in the United States being named the Great Satan and the enemy of the increasingly aggressive regime that replaced it. The implications of this continue to affect global politics, as can be seen in today's tense relationship between the United States and Iran.

Abel was a skilled and careful agent. Even when his agents were exposed, his cover was never blown. Two of his agents, the husband-and-wife team Morris and Ilona Cohen, had to disappear in 1950 for fear of arrest, but the Russians simply sent them to England, where they continued spying under the new aliases of Peter and Helen Kroger until they were eventually caught when the Portland spy ring was unmasked in 1964.

However, Abel's masters made a fatal blunder in 1953 when they appointed Reino Hayhanen to work as Abel's contact with his own service. Hayhanen was a disaster. He neglected his espionage and liaison duties and spent his time drinking and womanising – paid for by stealing from network funds. In 1957 he was ordered back to Moscow but broke his journey in Paris, where he called at the US embassy and announced his defection. Interviewed by the CIA, he put the investigators on the trail of his case officer, a Soviet spy named Mark, operating without diplomatic cover and

Russian spies Peter and Helen Kroger walk out to a Warsaw-bound aircraft at Heathrow Airport in 1969 after being released from a twenty-year jail sentence for their part in the Portland Spy Ring, in exchange for British spy Gerald Brooke.

Francis Gary Powers with a model of his U-2 plane, testifying in Washington before a Senate Committee. Powers was exchanged for Russian spy Rudolf Abel in 1962.

under several false identities. After painstaking detective work, agents figured out that Mark was in fact Colonel Rudolf Abel, who was arrested on 21 June 1957. Although Abel refused to talk, his hotel room and office revealed an important prize: a treasure trove of modern espionage equipment. Further evidence was provided by Master Sergeant Roy Rhodes, an American spy also betrayed by Hayhanen, who had worked for the Russians during his time at the US embassy in Moscow. He also knew Abel's false identity.

Abel himself was tried and convicted of espionage but was finally exchanged in 1962 for Francis Gary Powers, the American pilot of the U-2 spy plane that had been shot down over Russia two years before. After his return to Moscow he continued to work as a trainer for the KGB and was rewarded with the Order of Lenin.

SPYMASTERS & MASTER SPIES
The Costs of Direct Action

Spies operating in a war zone suffer additional problems in an already dangerous job – from becoming a casualty of military action to the heightened risk of discovery as a result of stronger defences and increased public suspicion of strangers. Nevertheless, all countries have used spies in active operations, from the assassination of hostile leaders or agents on the enemy side to the triggering of military operations up to and including full-scale invasions.

Direct action normally makes sense at the time. In the longer term, though, it can be extremely counterproductive. For example, the German spymaster Captain Franz von Rintelen infiltrated the United States on a Swiss passport in 1915 to start a sabotage campaign. He fell into violent disagreement with German diplomats in America who were worried that his activities risked prejudicing their interests in what was still a neutral country.

In the end their fears were justified by disasters like the great ammunition explosion at Black Tom Island, a pier on the Jersey City waterfront opposite the Statue of Liberty. At 2:08 a.m. on 31 July 1916, a huge explosion, followed by many smaller detonations, destroyed some thousand tonnes of

The aftermath of a series of massive explosions at the Black Tom Island munitions facility in New Jersey, 30 July 1916.

ammunition in barges and railway wagons destined for transport to the Allies in Europe. The depot was completely destroyed, with property damage of more than $20 million. Windows were shattered in Lower Manhattan and the Statue of Liberty itself was peppered with fragments from the explosion, causing damage up to $100,000.

This and other fires and explosions at foundries and factories in the eastern United States had negligible effect on the huge quantities of war materials being shipped to Germany's opponents. The sabotage campaign, however, succeeded in alienating American public opinion, so that later moves by Germany against US interests (see Zimmermann Telegram, page 96) helped tilt the balance from initial hostility to a declaration of war in 1917.

Sidney Reilly

Another shadowy figure whose legacy turned sour was self-styled master spy Sidney Reilly, who operated in Russia before and after the 1917 Bolshevik Revolution. Even his name is uncertain – he stated that he was the son of a Russian mother and an Irish father who was skipper of a merchant ship, but others insisted he had been born Georgi (or Sigmund) Rosenblum to a Jewish doctor father and an Irish Catholic mother, and this was certainly a cover he adopted at one time. He also claimed to have been involved in a British plot to murder Lenin and Trotsky, and he was later implicated in the 'Zinoviev letter' deception (see Espionage in Action, pages 96–97). Whatever the truth, his involvement in the unstable early days of the Soviet Union caused a long and deep distrust in the minds of Russian leaders for the nations of the West.

British master spy Captain Sidney Reilly claims to have been involved in a plot to murder Lenin and Trotsky.

Brutal reprisals

In World War II brave and effective direct-action campaigns triggered terrible reprisals from the Nazis. In occupied Czechoslovakia in 1942, a well-aimed bomb took the life of Reinhard Heydrich en route to his Prague office in an open-top Mercedes. He was Reichsprotektor of the annexed provinces of Bohemia and Moravia and was chiefly responsible for the extermination of the Jews there. The Germans hunted down and shot the agents who had killed him, but this was merely the beginning. The Czech population were punished by the obliteration of the village of Lidice and the murder of its inhabitants, a fate also meted out to the French village of Oradour-sur-Glane when French Resistance agents tried to impede the movement of the second SS Panzer Division 'Das Reich' from its base in southern France on its way to attack the Allied bridgehead in Normandy in June 1944.

ESPIONAGE IN ACTION
The value of forgeries

Engaging in spying fosters a culture of secrecy and deceit, so that countries tend to suspect both adversaries and allies of underhand conduct. In this atmosphere of paranoia, fragments of information can be accepted at face value or denied as deliberate attempts to mislead. In two cases, one true and one false, documents have had a powerful effect quite beyond that intended by those responsible for writing them: the 'Zinoviev Letter' and the 'Zimmerman Telegram'.

The Zinoviev Letter

The Zinoviev letter was a clever forgery produced in 1924 by a group of Russian émigrés who fled to the West after the Bolshevik Revolution. They wanted to alert British public opinion to the dangers of Communist infiltration and Russian attempts to export their revolution to the democratic governments of Europe. The group published a letter apparently signed by Grigori Zinoviev, president of Communist International, instructing British comrades to work undercover for the Labour Party, with the ultimate aim of bringing about the longed-for revolution. The text was published in British newspapers just four days before the 1924 General Election, and produced a sharp change in predicted voting patterns. The Conservatives were swept back to power and Labour remained in opposition, while the fall-out created a deeper freeze in relations between Britain and the Soviet Union.

The Zimmerman Telegram

Another document with even more powerful effects was sent by the German Foreign Office to Count Von Bernstorff, the Kaiser's Ambassador to the United States, on 16 January 1917. Signed by Foreign Minister Arthur Zimmermann, it asked the ambassador to contact his opposite number in Mexico and instruct him to give the Mexican president the following message:

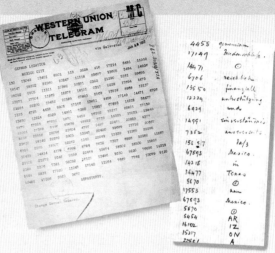

The Zimmerman Telegram (left) and the decoded text (right).

We intend to begin on 1st February unrestricted submarine warfare. We shall endeavor in spite of this to keep the United States of America neutral. In the event of this not succeeding, we make Mexico a proposal of alliance on the following basis: Make war together, make peace together, generous financial support and an understanding on our part that Mexico is to re-conquer the lost territory in Texas, New Mexico, and Arizona.

You will inform the President of the above most secretly as soon as the outbreak of war with the United States is certain and add the suggestion that he should, on his own initiative, invite Japan to immediate adherence and at the same time mediate between Japan and ourselves. Please call the President's attention to the fact that the ruthless employment of our submarines now offers the prospect of compelling England in a few months to make peace.

Unrestricted submarine warfare against merchant shipping bound for Britain was provocative enough to

the United States, but the idea of backdoor offers of American territory to Mexico was potential dynamite. The British had already deciphered the text of this new document using the code-breakers at Room 40 in the Admiralty. But how could they reveal its text to the Americans without their assuming it was a forgery and without revealing to the Germans that the British had cracked their diplomatic cipher?

The declaration of war

The solution was to search for the cable that Bernstorff would have reenciphered in order to forward it to the German ambassador in Mexico City, as this was bound to differ in some details from the original message. It would also be sent in a lower-grade cipher than the original Diplomatic Code. If the British revealed they had broken this cipher, it was less likely the Germans would go to the trouble of

A German U-boat opens fire on an Allied merchant ship in the North Atlantic during World War I (c. 1915).

changing all their higher-grade diplomatic ciphers as well. Finally the enciphered text of this message was found in the Mexico City office of Western Union by a British agent code-named T.

When deciphered, the text was found to carry a different date, serial number, and instructions from the original Zimmermann Telegram. This text was shown to a US diplomat in London, who was allowed to witness the deciphering process under supervision, to prove the message was genuine. When the news broke in America, the Germans began an official enquiry, virtually admitting the message was genuine. War fever in the United States finally triggered the declaration of war on Germany on 6 April 1917. Allied victory was now virtually guaranteed.

From a Safe Distance

Signals Intelligence – shortened to SIGINT – involves the interception and analysis of communications, including decryption of coded messages, direction finding and traffic analysis. With further development of electronics technology, ELINT – Electronic Intelligence – extended these techniques into the analysis of the wider field of electronic emissions, including, for example, radar transmissions, infrared data, sound signals from submerged submarines and the sensor suites built into electronic surveillance satellites.

In the history of espionage one of the greatest single leaps forward in terms of technology was the invention of radio. From that moment, messages could no longer be intercepted by closing frontiers or arresting suspicious travellers. Radio signals reached their destinations almost instantaneously, and replies could be received within minutes. This helped spies in three ways.

1. They could stay in touch with their controllers at all times, without having to risk dangerous journeys to make reports in person.

2. They could ask for advice or assistance at any time.

3. With the right equipment they could listen to their enemies' radio messages – nothing broadcast could be kept secret from anyone with a receiver tuned to the right frequency.

This meant that spies' own communications were also insecure – any technology available to one side would be available to opposition espionage agents as well. This weakness of radio transmission led to the development of complex codes and ciphers to obscure the meaning of messages. Ingenious means of hiding the original message were used by all sides in an attempt to preserve the confidentiality of their communications (see Chapter 9).

NASA's Lockheed SR-71 aircraft (the 'Blackbird'), an advanced, long-range, strategic reconnaissance aircraft that was permanently retired in 1998.

Even without codebooks or cipher keys, spies can still deduce valuable information from the density of signals traffic, the length of messages, the locations of the transmitters and the characteristics of the call signs used to tell the recipient who had sent the original message.

What does it all mean?

During the days of the Cold War, when the massed forces of NATO and the Warsaw Pact faced one another across the Iron Curtain, each side was under constant threat of attack. This was a particular problem for NATO, facing the much larger conventional weapons resources of the Eastern bloc. This meant NATO forces had to keep a close watch on all Eastern bloc military signals. Any increase in the amount of traffic resulting from an upsurge in military activity was immediately apparent. Because treaties required both sides to give prior warning of any military exercises, NATO military intelligence also knew what sort of tactics would be used and how these would be reflected in radio traffic.

The intensity of traffic provided only basic intelligence. More detail was produced by accurate direction finding. Each message would be recorded by three or more monitoring stations, and in each case the bearing from each station would be noted. Plotting the bearings on a map and finding the common point would reveal the location of the sender of the message at the time of its transmission.

Call signs

Even without ciphers to decode the intercepted messages, important information could be deduced from the call signs used to identify the sender and the movements of the transmitter between successive signals. In most cases the letters and numbers of a call sign would mean nothing to those listening in, but particular units tended to use the same combination for all their messages. This would allow signals intelligence experts to count the number of messages sent by a particular unit and also to plot the positions from which successive signals were sent.

This would establish a pattern that might suggest the type of unit using a particular call sign. A transmitter that moved relatively large distances over short time intervals between successive signals, for example, might be an armoured unit or a light reconnaissance unit. Shorter movements hinted at infantry units, and relatively static transmitter positions could belong to artillery units or, depending on the amount of traffic, headquarters of larger formations like divisions or army corps.

Signals intelligence

Once this kind of information was retrieved, more could be deduced from signals intelligence. For example, armoured units would normally be the first to cross the East–West European frontier in the event of a full-scale attack. Therefore, if these units were operating close to the frontier, this could indicate an imminent attack. However, if they were merely involved in training exercises, their movements would take place farther back behind the frontier under a tight security blanket. Thus, the positions from which their transmissions were being sent provided an indicator of the likely threat level.

The amount of signals traffic and the number of different transmitters and unit call signs involved also showed the size of the forces being monitored. A small number of transmitters and positions relating to a small sector of the East–West frontier pointed to small-scale local operations. Very large numbers of transmitters from positions spread over hundreds of miles and close to the East–West border suggested a much larger operation that merited close attention.

Nothing in espionage, however, is simple, and signals intelligence is no exception. The senders of signals can also use their radio networks to pass on disinformation to mislead the opposite side. They can disguise units by changing their call signs. The Japanese Navy in World War II sent ciphered messages with battleship call signs from smaller ships, such as destroyers, to confuse US intelligence about Japanese movements and intentions. Another ploy was to send signals by landline to transmitters in a different location to mislead opposition direction-finding (see below).

Transmission deception

In October 1942, during the build up to the Battle of Alamein in World War II, the British Eighth Army was preparing to attack the German Afrika Corps commanded by Field Marshal Erwin Rommel in the Western Desert. The

The German military Tonschreiber tape recorder, developed in the 1930s, was used for a variety of purposes. Easy to transport in a field pack, it was an invaluable tool for recording programs, listening in on long-distance calls, and recording and broadcasting military propaganda.

INFORMATION
Accurate or Misleading?

Technical intelligence still suffers from one major limitation: it can reveal resources, locations, strengths and movements, but not plans and intentions. A good demonstration of both the limitations and possibilities of technical intelligence can be seen in the first Gulf War.

The day before Saddam Hussein mounted the 2 August 1990 invasion of Kuwait, technical intelligence surveillance, using satellite coverage and electronic sensors, showed his army units massing along the Kuwaiti border at threatening levels. However, what it could not show was whether an invasion was imminent or whether this was merely a crude attempt to bully Iraq's smaller neighbuor into strategic concessions.

Everything changed once the leading Iraqi troops crossed the frontier. At the very moment when human agents would find it impossible to relay information back to their controllers, technical intelligence went on reporting Iraqi troop movements, tactics, deployment of weapons and, in due course, the build-up of defences designed to make it difficult for coalition forces to liberate the country from Saddam Hussein's control.

Disinformation

In the later stages of the first Gulf War campaign, coalition forces were able to mislead the Iraqis over where and when their attacks would be delivered. Evidence suggesting that troops were being massed for a landing on Iraqi territory from the headwaters of the Gulf was made as obvious as possible. This included signals traffic, movements of warships, naval gunfire and coastal minesweeping in a carefully planned disinformation campaign. Meanwhile, in the vast desert to the west, coalition forces built up their strength unseen and unsuspected by Iraq, finally delivering a powerful attack with almost total surprise.

Dummy tanks

Not all deceptions have to be expensive or elaborate – sometimes the simplest can drastically affect opposition intelligence. During fighting in the Iraqi desert, US A10 tank-buster aircraft searched for Iraqi armoured vehicles with infrared detection. Any attempt to use a dummy tank to invite attacks and cause antitank missiles to be wasted would normally fail, because the pilot would see no infrared emissions from the 'tank'. Yet the Iraqis realised this weakness and managed to exploit it by placing cheap room heaters by each of their dummy defensive positions. The A10s spotted the heat source and the badly camouflaged 'tank' and wasted time and resources launching missiles at them.

The Falklands War

During the Argentine invasion of the Falkland Islands in 1982, a potential headache for the British was the threat of attack by the Argentine Navy. One reason why this never happened was a ruse by the helicopter of HMS *Endurance*, the Antarctic survey vessel patroling in the region. The helicopter crew followed a carefully planned course through fields of icebergs that made interception difficult at a speed similar to that of a surfaced nuclear submarine. They then carried out a radio conversation with their own ship, using a call sign that the Argentines would identify as belonging to one of the Royal Navy's nuclear-powered hunter-killer submarines, a deadly threat to any Argentine ships in the vicinity. The Argentine fleet therefore stayed bottled up in harbour at the start of the campaign when their presence might have made all the difference. Eventually their heavy cruiser, *General Belgrano*, emerged on a sortie, only to be intercepted and sunk by HMS *Conqueror*, a genuine hunter-killer that had completed the long passage from Britain while the Argentine forces were still reacting to the earlier (and imaginary) threat.

British wanted to mislead the Germans about where they would actually attack. The main assault was planned for the north, so it was important to suggest that the main focus of activity was in the south. The army signals transmitters were in the north, where the majority of the attacking units were based. By sending these signals down a landline to another transmitting station at the southern end of the front and broadcasting messages from there, the

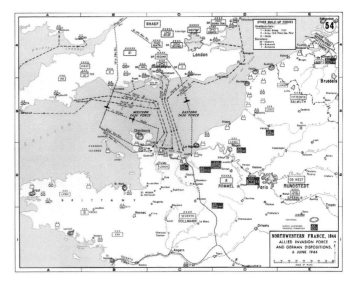

British were able to convince the German range-finding and traffic-analysis stations that the action would be launched in the south.

Later in the war, during the buildup to the D-Day Normandy landings in June 1944, an Allied deception plan was designed to make the Germans believe that the original landings were a feint to engage German forces, while the main landings were to be made farther east – across the narrowest part of the English Channel facing the Pas de Calais.

To make the plan seem feasible, the Allies leaked to the Germans the presence of a huge (though totally fictitious) formation called the First United States Army Group, or FUSAG, which was based in East Anglia. Additional buildings were constructed and dummy vehicles and landing craft were placed around possible embarkation points. To support this, a huge amount of false radio traffic was transmitted. In order to keep up the pretence that the troops were based in this area, all signals sent to the genuine landing forces, based in southwest England, were first relayed by landline to a transmitter in southeast England. Once again, German monitors and direction finders would assume from the position of the transmitter that this huge amount of still undeciphered radio traffic related to the (imaginary) FUSAG forces waiting to invade the Pas de Calais.

Operation Fortitude was a great success. The Germans positioned the majority of their troops in the Pas de Calais, with the result that Allied troops landing in Normandy encountered less resistance than they would otherwise have done. The disinformation campaign surrounding the Normandy landings undoubtedly had a huge impact on the eventual outcome of the war.

Map showing the Allied invasion plans for D-Day. Espionage activity meant that the Germans were expecting the invasion much farther to the east.

103

From a Safe Distance

Reconnaissance flights

A second great invention brought about another transformation in espionage. Where radio had allowed spies to listen in on their opponents' conversations, the aeroplane gave them the opportunity to watch them as well. Reconnaissance flights could pinpoint the positions of military bases, warships, fortifications, factories, railway networks and airfields. When aircraft were fitted with sophisticated cameras, the amount of information from a single sortie was magnified many times over. Intelligence workers became sensitive to changes in pictures taken on successive flights over a specific area. Comparing pictures could document changes in troop levels, buildup of fortifications, new types of aircraft or different disposition of naval units.

Photo-reconnaissance was first used in a major way during World War II. Previously, converted bombers had been used for airborne reconnaissance as

Tracking station of a US E-2C aircraft, used for surveillance.

Photo interpreters who are trained to notice even the smallest changes in a series of photographs play a vital role in any espionage network.

they were the only aircraft with a long enough range. However, from 1939 onwards aircraft such as the RAF's Spitfire and Mosquito began to be used instead. These smaller, faster aircraft could reach higher altitudes and were better at avoiding detection, and could therefore provide a greater volume of information. Collecting and interpreting the photographs was a considerable enterprise: at its peak, the British flew over 100 reconnaissance missions a day, providing the photo interpreters with over 50,000 images to examine.

This kind of espionage-at-arm's-length became invaluable for locations where placing human agents was all but impossible, such as the campaign against the German V2 rocket development programme (see page 76). During the Allies' final push against the Germans in 1944, the RAF used photo-reconnaissance to assess the Germans' strategic industries in order to plan their bombing campaign as accurately as possible.

ADDING ELINT TO THE PICTURE

As the stakes increased and technological advances were made, visual intelligence was soon joined by ELINT, or electronic intelligence, which covered electronic transmissions not directly involved with communications.

**USS *Lake Erie*,
equipped with a
powerful armament of
radar equipment used
to target its missiles.**

Radar

Radar was increasingly important in detecting
hostile aircraft and controlling missiles and
antiaircraft barrages designed to beat them
off. Even in peacetime it was vital to identify
gaps in the opposition's air-defence radar
coverage so that sorties could be sent in
undetected should hostilities break out. It was
also possible to block radar coverage if you
had access to a radar station's scan patterns
and transmission frequencies. This involved
jamming the station's radar, swamping it with
electronic interference or misleading it with spurious echoes made by
dropping metal foil in huge quantities.

Radar also identifies targets for antiaircraft missiles and often steers the
missiles to final impact. This happened both in North Vietnam and in Iraq
during the first Gulf War campaign in 1991. These radars can be jammed or
misled and even targeted by special anti-radar missiles launched from
incoming aircraft to home in on air-defence radar signals. Usually defenders
can detect the launch of these missiles, whereupon they switch off their
radars long enough for the antiradar missiles to lose their intended targets.
The secondary effect is that any antiaircraft missiles then being controlled by
that particular radar station also lose their targets. Since stocks of these
hugely expensive weapons are always limited, an entire air-defense system
could be crippled by just a few raiders with the smaller and cheaper
antiradar missiles and the right electronic intelligence to lead them to
their targets.

Enigma intercepts

Electronic intelligence has also been successful in reaching even further into
the other side's most secret sites and developments. When the German V1
cruise missile was being tested before being launched against southern England
from sites on the French coast, flights were made from Peenemunde out into
the Baltic Sea. There was no way to infiltrate agents into Peenemunde to
watch the missiles fired into sea areas far away from the coast.

Yet Enigma intercepts revealed that two specialist Luftwaffe signal
regiments had been posted to the area, and it was clear they would be used
to plot the speeds and ranges of the test missiles. By deciphering the range
and bearings quoted in their reports, intelligence experts in London had a
front-row view of the progressively improving accuracy of these weapons,

TECHNOLOGY
Listening to Submarines

Electronic intelligence is used to monitor the movements and capabilities of other nations' submarine forces. During World War II, submerged submarines were hunted by equipment called ASDIC by the British (derived from the Anti-Submarine Detection Investigation Committee, which developed the system) and sonar by the Americans. Sound pulses were sent through the water from a transmitter on board each submarine hunter. If a pulse hit the hull of a submerged submarine, it would rebound and be picked up. The bearing of the transmitter and the delay before the echo returned would give an approximate position for the submarine, which could then be attacked by depth charges.

Since then, this type of active sonar has very rarely been used because it gives the target far too much information on the presence and position of the vessel using it. Instead, passive sonar, which simply listens to the sounds made by the hostile submarine, has become universally adopted. However, this means a truly quiet submarine can be difficult or even impossible to detect.

As a result, all navies strive to reduce all sources of sound in their submarines. Everything from the profile of the propellers driving the submarine forward to noises like a spanner being dropped in the engine room, all have to be suppressed as the price for survival.

Until total quiet is reached, every submarine will produce a slightly different combination of sounds, depending on its propulsion, machinery mountings, hull shape and mechanical condition. By developing passive sonar equipment that can filter out and display the different components of a submarine's overall sound signature, experienced sonar operators can determine the nationality, class and even individual identity of a submarine.

This same principle has been extended to large fixed arrays of passive sonar equipment laid across natural choke points in the world's oceans, like the gaps between Greenland, Iceland and the UK that restrict access for Russian submarines in Arctic bases to reach the open oceans. The SOSUS (Sound Surveillance System) array that monitors these gaps can identify the details of each submarine crossing between their bases and their operational areas, information that can determine the threat level at any time.

From a Safe Distance

Electronic intelligence equipment being used on board the aircraft carrier USS *Kitty Hawk*.

together with the heights and speeds at which they flew – essential information for planning fighter patrols and antiaircraft batteries to bring them down. During the Cold War this ability to eavesdrop on opposition telemetry data – information sent back by missiles fired on test launches – enabled Western intelligence to follow the flight of Soviet missiles to determine their speed, range and numbers of warheads.

Infrared radiation

Infrared radiation is also a valuable source of information about opposition defences. It works by indicating the different levels of heat in a specific location, allowing agents to build up a thermal photograph of the area under surveillance, with hotter objects showing up in different shades from cooler objects. This enables the agent to see targets such as human beings and vehices, which will be hotter than the surrounding area. In this way, a reconnaissance plane over an air base can see which dispersal points held recently departed aircraft – indicated by the slight increase in warmth over the surrounding area. Infrared false-colour photography can also distinguish between live foliage and cut branches used to camouflage tanks or trenches.

Students studying radio equipment in a class at the German Luftwaffe Technical School in 1959.

SATELLITES FOR THE UNOBSTRUCTED VIEW

Finally, the most dramatic advance in espionage technology has been the invention of the satellite, orbiting the world without the old restrictions on national airspace that enabled the Russians to shoot down the American U-2 spy plane crossing their territory in 1960.

The development of satellites

The earliest satellites used film cameras that demanded a way of recovering the exposed film while the satellite continued its mission. Until the 1970s and even the 1980s, many reconnaissance satellites that took photographs would simply eject canisters of photographic film, which would descend to Earth and be retrieved in mid-air as they floated down on parachutes. However, the danger with this system was that any information gleaned from the satellite was in no way secure, because there was no guarantee who would pick up the photographs.

Later, satellites transmitted picture information through video cameras, together with data from electronics and infrared sensors. Most recently, satellites have been fitted with remote-control rockets that can alter their orbit to include closer coverage of particular regions and cameras sensitive enough to pick out single figures standing in the open – night or day.

Computer wizardry

So huge are the areas covered on each satellite orbit that thousands of miles of sea, forest or desert with little interest needs to be filtered out. How is this done? Computer software analyses the picture data and reacts to signs of deliberate construction – straight lines, sharp edges, regular angles – and devotes maximum concentration to those. With this eye-in-the-sky passing overhead at regular intervals, it has therefore become almost impossible for even the most secretive nations to keep new developments hidden. Now all they can hope to do is disguise or camouflage sensitive installations in order to mislead those who use satellite information for intelligence purposes.

The Internet

More recently, the sharp rise in the use of electronic communications over the Internet has given espionage services vast new data sets. Sophisticated listening devices and powerful mainframe computers make it possible to monitor this huge mass of information anywhere in the world and to pick out messages with keywords that suggest that crimes or acts of terrorism are being planned or executed.

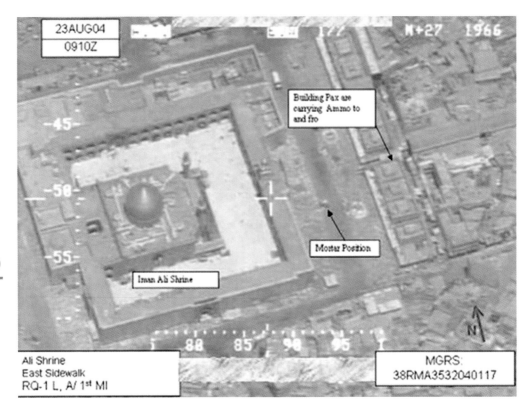

23AUG04
0910Z

N+27 1966

Building Pax are
carrying Ammo to
and fro

-45-

-50-

-55-

Mortar Position

Iman Ali Shrine

N

Ali Shrine
East Sidewalk
RQ-1 L, A/ 1st MI

MGRS:
38RMA3532040117

US Central Command surveillance photo of militia mortar positions in Najaf, Iraq, on 23 August 2004.

Surveying your competitors

The fact remains that this capability can be used for commercial as well as military advantages, and the United States has been accused of using information for the benefit of American firms competing with those of other nations. The French have complained bitterly about these alleged activities, but they too are guilty of such practices. For example, the former French intelligence chief Pierre Marion claimed his service intercepted American messages to reveal confidential information from US aircraft companies, enabling the French manufacturer Dassault to undercut the Americans and win important contracts.

Sharing your information

The United States and the United Kingdom have a long-established agreement to pool any information each country may receive from its surveillance activities. However, the European Union is currently trying to force Britain to share this: a campaign that, if successful, will put this agreement under severe strain.

TECHNOLOGY
Menwith Hill

Described as the biggest technical intelligence-monitoring site in the world, Menwith Hill in North Yorkshire is jointly operated by Britain's GCHQ (Government Communications Headquarters, one of the UK's intelligence-gathering and security organisations) and the American NSA (National Security Agency). With a staff of almost two thousand people, its chief landmarks are the twenty-seven spherical covers for the satellite dishes and aerial arrays used to monitor signals all over the world. These include microwave telephone links picked up by satellites and relayed to the site. In 1977 newspaper reports claimed these facilities had recorded a car-phone conversation between Soviet leader Leonid Brezhnev and his defence minister about hiding new weapons in old locations to gain an advantage in arms-reduction talks with the United States.

With the ending of the Cold War, the Hill's awesome monitoring capabilities have shifted to new targets. Current priorities include checking evidence of rogue states sponsoring terrorist organisations or backing terrorist operations, or the development of weapons of mass destruction. Other targets include moving large sums of money through the world banking system by terrorist paymasters or organised crime syndicates.

Perhaps the best tribute to the effectiveness of electronic intelligence was the report that the successors to the Soviet KGB – which always depended more on human agents and less on technical intelligence than its Western counterparts – have been rapidly catching up. The Russians unexpectedly killed the Chechnyan rebel leader, General Dzokhar Dudayev, on 21 April 1966. He was in the open, speaking on a satellite phone to one of his associates when he was killed by an air-launched missile. Russian news sources insist that his calls had been intercepted and monitored and that the missile homed in on his personal phone signals.

ABOVE Aerial photograph of the Menwith Hill monitoring station near Harrogate in North Yorkshire, UK. This base is operated by the US National Security Agency.

BELOW The spherical cover of one of the satellite dishes at Menwith Hill.

Codes and Ciphers

At one time spies would memorise vital information and pass it on by word of mouth. More and more complex data, however, made severe demands on the memory, and verbally relaying secret information exposed the agent to the threat of capture and interrogation. Sending messages was safer but required codes or ciphers to obscure the meaning from the enemy. In today's electronic era, powerful digital encryption protects data against criminals. Some encryption, in fact, is so ingenious that it still remains unsolved.

A cipher text bears a regular relationship to the actual message, or plaintext. In a substitution cipher, for example, every letter of the plaintext will be represented by a different letter in the cipher text. Coded messages use a different kind of protection: Code words known to both sender and receiver are substituted for words or phrases in the original message.

Depending on the range of information being sent, codes can be simple or complex. If a spy knows that the information needed has to do with whether or not the enemy fleet has sailed, then only two different code words are needed: effectively, yes or no. Provided both the agent and those receiving the message know those are the only two options, then including either word in the message will give it away. In practice, messages convey more information – 'returning home on Tuesday' might mean the enemy fleet is preparing to sail, while 'staying another week' might mean no preparations are being made.

The chief problem with coded messages arises with information not covered by the list of codes in the possession of both agent and spymaster. The original enemy fleet may not leave harbour, for example. Instead, another task force may arrive to add to the original fleet's strength. When this larger force sails, it presents a communication problem for the spy – how can he or she describe the change in fleet strength when using a code that has no phrase for that?

Rotors used in the Enigma machine, the cipher system used by the Germans during WWII.

Codes, however elaborate, sooner or later must deal with words that have no equivalent in the codebook. Because ciphers simply transpose letters, they can express the most complex information. Unfortunately, this is also their major drawback: Once counterintelligence has worked the cipher out, it can decipher the whole message with ease.

UNRAVELLING CIPHER TEXT

Cipher traffic boomed with the invention of radio, which greatly simplified contact between agents and their controllers back at headquarters. It also made it possible for the hundreds of thousands of signals needed to run navies, armies and air forces in modern warfare to be sent much more reliably and quickly. This meant that a secure cipher method was needed to cope with huge volumes of traffic, managed by equipment carried in every signals office and aboard every ship.

The major weakness of any regular cipher system, with a fixed relationship between plaintext and cipher text, is that it can be broken by frequency analysis. Usually, in English texts 'e' is the most common letter, followed by 'a', then 't' and so on. Counting the frequencies with which individual letters appear in cipher text exposes the relationships between plaintext and cipher text. For example, if 'x' appears most frequently in the cipher text, then it probably represents 'e'. Similar rules apply to other languages, making it possible to break messages sent in a regular cipher in German or Russian as well as English.

The cipher wheel

One way of avoiding this weakness is to change the relationship between cipher letters and plaintext letters several times in a message. In the late fifteenth century the Florentine cryptologist Leon Battista Alberti invented the cipher wheel to do this. This ingenious method of encryption used a disc with all twenty-six letters of the alphabet arranged in a jumbled order around its circumference. This was pinned to a larger disc that also had the alphabet printed around its circumference, and the two discs could be rotated relative to one another. The cipher to be used was signaled by the first two letters of a particular message. If these read 'sx', for example, then the recipient of the message knew it was essential to set the discs so that the letter 's' on the outer disc was aligned with letter 'x' on the inner disc. This relationship allowed a text to be enciphered (and deciphered at the other end) using the relative positions of letters on the smaller and larger discs to translate between cipher text and plaintext.

Up to this point, of course, the encrypted message could still be broken by frequency analysis. However, Alberti's ground-breaking invention was to include a capital letter at intervals in the message. If the letter 'B' appeared in the cipher text, it was a signal to the recipient to realign the discs so that 'b' on the outer disc was now opposite 'x' on the inner disc, and so on. This shift could be carried out several times in the course of a message, making it much more difficult to decipher. Each new position of the discs brought new correlations between the encrypted text and the decoded texts, meaning the word 'cat' might have been 'gdi' in one instance, and 'alx' in another. The usefulness of frequency analysis was therefore greatly diminished.

In order to make the message still more difficult to crack, agents can use numbers on the outer ring as a kind of enciphered code. That is, before enciphering the message, he or she would substitute certain phrases with combinations of the numbers from 1 to 4, according to a small codebook. Those numbers would then be enciphered along with the rest of the message.

Telegram operators working at desks in 1963.

TECHNOLOGY
Nelson's signal at Trafalgar

Codes had to become more complex to cover different situations. Navies, for example, sometimes needed to send orders to all the ships in a fleet so they could act together quickly. Here the problem was speed more than security, but the solution was similar. Sending a detailed message with each signal flag standing for a single letter in a long and detailed message would take too long. Instead, each ship had a signal codebook.

Each single flag had a specific number from one to ten. When hoisted on its own, each number had its own meaning – for example, 1 meant 'Enemy in sight'. Longer numerical combinations meant specific words or phrases – 42 stood for 'the Admiralty', 56 signified 'America', and 2027 meant 'I have been in action'. Words not included could be spelled using the numerical equivalents of letters of the alphabet – numbers 1 and 2 hoisted together stood for the twelfth letter of the alphabet, or 'L', but this was laborious and avoided wherever possible.

The best example was Nelson's famous signal at the Battle of Trafalgar in October 1805. He originally intended to send 'Nelson confides that every man will do his duty'. It was pointed out that both the first and second words of the signal would need to be spelled out letter by letter, whereas 'England' and 'expects' existed in the codebook as simple three-flag combinations. The word 'duty', on the other hand, had no entry in the codebook, and spelling it out

Horatio Nelson, who famously used flags to encode the message 'England expects every man will do his duty' at the Battle of Trafalgar in 1805.

letter by letter called for seven separate flags out of the twenty-two for the whole signal. The final message, of course, became 'England expects every man will do his duty'.

THE FORMIDABLE POWER OF MACHINE CIPHERS

This basic principle was used in the development of cipher machines, changing the relationship between each letter and the next, making the cipher theoretically impossible to crack. During World War II the Germans used the Enigma cipher system, and the Japanese used a similar encryption method with their 'Purple' machine. The Enigma system described below demonstrates both.

How Enigma worked

The Enigma machine was a portable encryption machine about the same size as the processor unit of a desktop computer. A keyboard at the front of the machine was used to type in the message. Above the keyboard was a series of 26 lamps, each showing a letter of the alphabet. When a key was pressed, one of the lamps lit up, showing what that letter needed to be replaced with in the encrypted text. The letters were then noted by a second operator, who then sent the encrypted message using Morse code. These messages were then picked up by the intended recipients, who typed them into their own Enigma machine, set up in the same way as the sender's, and obtained the original message.

If the Enigma operator typed the letter 'a', then, depending on the initial settings of the machine, the lamp bearing the letter 't' might light up. However, thanks to three internal rotors, pressing the key would cause the first cipher wheel to move on by one position, so that pressing the 'a' key again would cause the current to follow a different path. This time the 'f' lamp might light, and the next time the 'm' light, and so on. The cipher relationship changed on each stroke of the key.

What made the Enigma machine truly alarming to the enemy was the

The Enigma machine, used by the Germans to encode messages in World War II. The Allies managed to break the code after capturing one of the machines, giving them access to Germany's 'secret' communications.

German soldiers enciphering a message using an Enigma machine in World War II.

number of different combinations that could link each plaintext letter with its cipher equivalent. With a particular set of discs and plug-board connections, the initial relationship would only repeat itself after 16,900 keystrokes. With most messages limited to a maximum of 250 letters, repetition could be avoided. The message was protected further by the large number of different settings before a signal was sent. The operator had to connect a series of specific sockets on the plug board to other numbered sockets, each connection changing the route that the current would follow when a key was pressed. In addition, a set of three discs from a total of five, each with different internal wiring, had to be fitted into the machine in specific positions, and then each disc had to be rotated to a specified starting position. It is estimated that there were 158 million million million possible different ways of setting up the machine at the beginning of the enciphering process. All these settings were laid out in tables issued to units and offices using Enigma machines – essential for deciphering Enigma signals. If even one of the variables was incorrect, an attempt to decipher the text produced gibberish.

When the machine breaks down

Yet this machine-controlled operation had its failings. Whatever plaintext letter was typed, an identical letter in the cipher text would never be produced – however many times the 'a' key was pressed, it would never light the 'a' lamp. Furthermore, if the 'a' in plaintext was equivalent to 'g' in cipher text, the same was true in reverse – the 'g' in plaintext would produce 'a' in cipher text.

Though the number of possible combinations was still enormous, these small chinks in the security armour eventually led to messages being deciphered by a group of brilliant, if eccentric, mathematicians and academics at Bletchley Park. This Victorian mansion (opposite) in Buckinghamshire, England, had been requisitioned by the British government for use as the Government Code and Cipher School. Essential to this deciphering success, particularly for the even more complex naval Enigma used by German U-boats (with four discs in the machine chosen from a set of eight, all with different internal wiring) was the theft of the setting tables and other information from German warships at sea (see Chapter 11).

LEFT Cryptographers at work in Hut 3 at Bletchley Park, where top-secret German military communications were deciphered during World War II.

BELOW Bletchley Park, Britain's intelligence headquarters during World War II.

Limitations of Enigma intelligence

Enigma intelligence had two major limitations. Firstly, taking action based on Enigma intercepts risked revealing to the Germans that their ciphers had been broken. The Germans would therefore change their enciphering messages, which would mean all the hard work by the team at Bletchley Park would be wasted. So there always had to be another convincing explanation available for any Allied action that was based on Enigma intelligence. When U-boats were attacked and sunk using their position reports, ciphered through the Enigma system, the Allies claimed the successes were due to advanced Allied direction-finding services. Because Allied DF techniques were often successful, the Germans continued to believe their ciphers were unbreakable, so the Allies continued to read them.

The second limitation was that only Enigma messages transmitted by radio could be read. The Germans sent messages by mail or landline in Occupied Europe, and these remained out of the Allies' reach.

'Purple', the Japanese cipher machine used in World War II.

The intelligence war against Japan

In contrast with the German communications, the signals traffic of the Japanese, routed over the vast empty spaces of the Pacific Ocean, was sent almost entirely by radio and therefore came under the scrutiny of the American cipher breakers. The cipher machine used by the Japanese was known as 'Purple' to the US army, and the Japanese thought that its encoded messages were unbreakable.

However, an ambitious and successful intelligence operation, code-named 'Magic' by the United States, deciphered the Japanese cipher system. Its efforts actually warned the United States of the buildup that led to the Japanese surprise attack on Pearl Harbor. On December 7, 1941, a Purple-encrypted message intercepted from the Japanese Embassy breaking off

TECHNOLOGY
German Success in the Naval Cipher War

Breaking the German Enigma ciphers gave the Allies a priceless advantage in the Battle of the Atlantic, but the first success in the intelligence campaign was scored by the Germans. Early in the war the German Beobachtungs-Dienst 'Observation Service', or B-Dienst, succeeded in cracking many of the ciphers used by the Royal Navy, which enabled the smaller, German fleet to evade contact with their much more powerful opponents. This greatly influenced the naval war. German surface raiders could evade the task forces searching for them, since deciphered signals revealed British positions and intentions. During the summer of 1940 German intelligence pinpointed the positions of six British submarines off the Danish coast; German antisubmarine forces sank all of them.

British officers on the bridge of a destroyer keep a lookout for German U-boats during the Battle of the Atlantic.

This advantage proved even more useful in the German invasion of Norway in the spring of 1940. The German Navy was concerned that British warships might threaten the troop transports of their invasion force heading for southern Norway, so the Germans sent a naval task force north toward Narvik as a decoy. The B-Dienst intercepted British signals, demonstrating that they had taken the bait and sent their warships northward, so the German landings in the south went ahead virtually unopposed.

Tracking convoys
The B-Dienst's finest success involved eavesdropping on the routing instructions for convoys between Britain and North America. After a German surface raider captured a British merchant ship in July 1940, the Germans seized a copy of the Allied Merchant Ships' Code, with the cipher tables used to protect messages written in the basic code. Other captured British merchantmen yielded more and more cipher information, so by 1941 the B-Dienst could read most of the instructions to merchant ship captains of the routes their convoys were to follow. Wolf packs of German submarines were then sent into those waters.

By the spring of 1943 more U-boats were in the Atlantic and more convoys were being located by intercepting British signals. Fortunately for the Allies, the German Naval Enigma system had been broken, and they could read the German signals in turn. The Royal Navy ciphers had been changed in August 1940, but the merchant ship signals were still wide open to the Germans. Thanks to Enigma, however, the Allies could divert convoys once they knew submarines were being sent to intercept them. The Germans would intercept the diversion orders and redirect the U-boats, whereupon the Allies would then order another diversion, and so on across the Atlantic.

The Allies finally defeated the U-boats with more escorts, more powerful weapons and more highly trained crews using more effective evasion tactics. The cipher war remained a hard-fought campaign on both sides because reading enemy signals was essential to maintaining the balance of power.

diplomatic relations with the United States was decrypted. It did not, however, reveal the target in time for the United States to take defensive action.

Magic did provide priceless intelligence in the Battle of Midway in June 1942, which changed the balance of power in the Pacific war in a single day. From early 1942, American communications intelligence had indicated that the Japanese had plans to expand further to the east, and on March 4 the designator 'AF' begain to appear in partially decoded messages. Finally, on 13 March, American cryptanalysts broke the Japanese Navy's code and identified 'AF' as Midway Island. This allowed the United States to prepare for the battle well in advance.

However, perhaps the most dramatic of Magic's successes came when it allowed a precisely planned air strike to assassinate the Imperial Japanese Navy's commander in chief across 965 kilometres (600 miles) of enemy territory (see page 125).

American Navy bombers fly over a burning Japanese ship during the Battle of Midway, 4 June 1942.

ONE-TIME PADS – THE UNCRACKABLE CIPHER?

Remarkably, the most unbreakable and successful cipher is also the simplest. All it requires is a series of sheets of printed paper bound into a 'one-time pad' (OTP). First used as long ago as 1917, each sheet of an OTP contains a series of random numbers grouped into three- or five-digit blocks, with each pad, each page and each row of numbers clearly marked.

They can be used in several ways, though the principle is the same. The sender of the message and the recipient each have a copy of the pad. One version involves the sender writing out the message to be transmitted, and then enciphering it by using the numbers on the top line of the top page of the OTP to modify the letters according to the random numbers. For example, if the first word of the message is 'attack' and the first two blocks of random numbers read '71243' and '59324', then the first character of the plaintext 'a' will be shifted seven places in the alphabet to produce the letter 'h' in the cipher text. In the same way, the first 't' will be moved one place, giving 'u' in the cipher text. The second 't' will be shifted two places, giving 'v', and so on. The complete word 'attack' will appear in cipher text as 'huvefp', and because each of these characters has been selected using completely random numbers, there is no underlying system for cipher-crackers to attack.

Other methods first transpose the plaintext message into a series of numbers and then change those numbers by adding or subtracting the random numbers on the OTP. Here the cipher text will end up as a series of numbers, which can be further encrypted for greater protection. The KGB relied on this method, and often the first group of numbers of a new message would tell the recipient the pad number, page number and line number as a protection against mistakes. To anyone not in possession of the right OTP – and individual agents were usually given their own individual OTPs to guard against one being discovered and used to decipher messages sent to or from colleagues – the message was completely secure. Throughout the cold war, Western intelligence never broke a message enciphered through an OTP.

TODAY'S CIPHER MACHINES

More recently, computers have been used to generate and break ciphers much more quickly and effectively than was possible with wartime technology. Remarkably, the one-time pad remains supreme, and careful agents can even disguise the fact that ciphers are being used at all. For example, codebooks can be concealed within a volume that accords perfectly with the agent's cover story and thus avoids suspicion. In other cases, the figures of a one-time pad can be concealed as accounts or production statistics in an apparently innocent official report.

Key settings secrets

The US Navy used Enigma-type machines in the late 1960s. The KL-47, for example, used a series of rotors set to different positions for enciphering and deciphering messages, and US traitor John Walker sold the key settings for this machine to the Russians in December 1967 (see Chapter 12). Later he provided them with details of the more sophisticated KW-7 cipher machine, which would have enabled them to read highly secret American Navy communications.

In January 1968 the North Koreans seized the US Navy communications ship *Pueblo* off their coast. They kept the crew in captivity for more than a year, interrogating and torturing them to gain information. They also stole the ship's KW-7 cipher machine, which was passed on to the Soviets. However, experience with Enigma showed that possessing the machine is virtually useless without the key settings and cipher tables, and changing these would plug the security breach. In this case, however, Walker's treachery gave the Russians sixteen years' access to American communications at the highest level – perhaps over a million signals revealing naval operational plans for the Vietnam war and tactics for tracking and identifying Soviet nuclear submarines.

Rotor-based machines such as this were largely replaced in the 1970s by systems such as the KL-51, which use digital electronics rather than rotors to encrypt the message. However, KL-7 machines were kept in service as backups and for special uses before eventually being withdrawn from service in June 1983.

The TSEC/KL-7, code-named ADONIS, was a rotor machine encryption system introduced in the 1950s by the NSA. It used eight rotors, seven of which moved in a complex pattern, to encrypt messages.

ESPIONAGE IN ACTION
Eavesdropping on the enemy

Admiral Isoruku Yamamoto commanded the Imperial Japanese Navy during World War II and was a major target for the United States. In the spring of 1943 he was directing heavy Japanese air attacks against American targets in the Solomon Islands and New Guinea. To boost morale among the units involved, he was to visit airfields on Bougainville and the surrounding islands. Orders were sent to local commanders, and the US radio intelligence service at Pearl Harbour picked up a signal at 5:55 P.M. on 13 April 1943, which was partly deciphered and translated to read:

> **From: CinC South-Eastern Air Fleet**
> **On 18 April CinC Combined Fleet [Yamamoto] will visit RXZ, R?? and RXP in accordance with following schedule.**
> **1. Depart RR at 0600 in a medium attack plane escorted by 6 fighters. Arrive RXZ at 0800. Proceed by minesweeper to R?? arriving at 0840. (_____ have minesweeper ready at ? base). Depart R?? at 0945 in above minesweeper, and arrive RXZ at 1030?....... Depart RXZ at 1100? in medium attack plane and arrive RXP at 1110. Depart RXP at 1400 in medium attack plane and arrive RR at 1540.**
> **2. At each of the above places the Commander-in-Chief will make short tour of inspection and at _____ he will visit the sick and wounded, but current operations should continue**

Cracking the code
The three-letter codes were locations, and the agents identified RR as the Japanese base at Rabaul on the island of New Britain, and RXZ as Ballale, a base on a small island off Bougainville, while RXP was Buin at the southern tip of Bougainville proper. Clearly, Yamamoto planned to land at Ballale airfield at 8:00 A.M. on 18 April and board the minesweeper at the nearby harbour. During the final stages of this flight, he would be just within range of a squadron of

Lockheed P38 Lightning fighters based at Henderson Field on the island of Guadalcanal more than 500 miles (800 km) away. Given Yamamoto's known obsession with punctuality, this gave the United States a slim chance of killing the most formidable enemy commander at very little risk.

The mission
Eighteen aircraft, all of them from 339 Squadron USAF, were fitted with every long-range fuel tank available on the island to permit a round-trip of more than 1,600 km (1,000 miles) to intercept Yamamoto's plane. Their target took off in a twin-engined bomber at exactly 6:00 A.M. from Rabaul, together with another bomber carrying his chief of staff, Admiral Ugaki, and an escort of the formidable Japanese Zero fighters. The P38s had departed thirty-five minutes earlier. One crashed on takeoff, and another aborted with fuel-tank problems, but the remaining sixteen headed for Bougainville island.

Arriving over the objective, the American pilots were elated to see a small formation approaching on schedule. Spotting two Japanese bombers where only one had been expected, the P38s split into three groups. Eight tackled the Japanese escorts, while the two remaining pairs went for one of the bombers each. It was all over in minutes – one of the bombers crashed into the sea with one wing ablaze; the other plunged into the forest. Ugaki escaped from the bomber that had crashed into the sea and swam ashore, but when troops cut their way to the wreckage of the other bomber in the forest, they found the body of their commander in chief.

An intelligence success
The P38s all returned safely to base, and the prearranged signal 'Pop goes the weasel' went out to all American commanders in that part of the Pacific. Their toughest adversary was dead betrayed by cipher weaknesses and by his own punctuality.

Using the Information

The bravest and most successful spies can deliver a flood of valuable information, more so than ever with modern technology, but that value can be realised only through proper analysis. Unfortunately, such analysis is often missing because headquarters are too cautious or too suspicious, and, as a result, intelligence may not be given its true value. Espionage history abounds with occasions where accurate information that contradicted the preconceptions of those in power was simply disbelieved and discounted.

Perhaps the most catastrophic example of a refusal to take first-class intelligence at its true value dates back to the titanic struggle between Hitler's Germany and Stalin's Russia in 1941. At the time, the Soviet dictator had one of the world's best espionage networks. He had stolen a jump on the West by signing a treaty with Hitler on the eve of the invasion of Poland in September 1939. This gave Russia almost half of Poland and saved Hitler from worrying about Britain and France striking a deal with Stalin to squeeze Germany between two fronts.

By the spring of 1941, however, the picture had changed dramatically. Hitler had conquered and occupied most of Europe. Britain stood alone, unable to pose a direct threat to Germany on her own. Meanwhile, the Nazis had their eye on Russia, the ultimate adversary in the struggle between Fascism and Communism that had been brewing for more than a decade. Hitler was building up huge armies on Russia's borders, and the invasion was imminent. Fortunately, Stalin's agents in Europe and the Far East had informed him of what was happening in plenty of time to take counteraction. Less happily, he chose to ignore their messages.

The Soviet Red Orchestra
What German counterintelligence called the 'Rote Kapelle' or the 'Red Orchestra' was the core of the Soviet spy network in Western Europe. The

Satellite image taken on 18 October 2000, of the Al Qaim nuclear facility in Iraq. This facility was completely destroyed during the 1991 Gulf War, but this image indicates that the facility had been rebuilt, leading to speculation that Iraq was secretly stockpiling uranium here.

NKVD, as the Soviet secret police was then called, had set up a series of spy rings. The most important was a network run by Leopold Trepper. He was sent to Brussels in the spring of 1939, posing as a Canadian businessman eager to sell a line of umbrellas overseas. After the Germans conquered France and the Low Countries, he set up two new companies, based in Paris and Brussels, to sell black-market goods to the Germans. This gave Trepper and his agents access to high-level German contacts, producing priceless information on German resources, plans and intentions.

Richard Sorge, trained as an agent by the Russians, was even more successful. Posing as a journalist, he was sent to Tokyo in 1933, where he established a spy ring that penetrated both the German embassy and the Japanese government, giving him access to the most secret information through chief agent Ozaki Hozumi, a Japanese journalist and government adviser whom he had met in Shanghai several years before.

Legendary Soviet secret agent Richard Sorge was exposed and executed in Japan in 1944.

Stalin blind to Nazi threat

Two weeks before Hitler invaded Russia, Sorge sent Moscow details of the German buildup along the Soviet frontier, including the date of the planned attack, the German Wehrmacht's strategy and its military objectives. Stalin was unconvinced and ignored the intelligence, just as he had Western warnings that Hitler would attack the Soviet Union sooner or later. Stalin disregarded all the warnings he received – not only from Sorge and the West but also from his own agents in Europe, including the Red Orchestra. He trusted his 'intuition' and was convinced Hitler would not attack, that he had signed an eternal pact of friendship with Germany. So the dispatches from Japan and Europe, together with all others suggesting an imminent German attack, were buried in the files. And at 3:30 A.M. on 22 June 1941, Russian trains loaded with grain, ore, rubber, and fuel were crossing the border into German territory to maintain

deliveries of war material specified in the Nazi–Soviet pact. At that moment, German artillery launched a furious barrage, and a vast army more than a hundred divisions strong crossed the frontier on a 1,600 km (1,000-mile) front, from the Black Sea in the south to the Baltic in the north.

Soviet planes sitting in rows on their airfields were destroyed by German air raids. Red Army units radioed to their headquarters that they were under fire and were told they must be insane and were criticised for not putting their signals in code. Stalin's conviction that a German attack was fiction ruled the day and, when it came, surprised the Russians as much as the Germans had hoped it would.

A lesson learned

Stalin proved to be a fast learner. When six months later – with the Germans so close to Moscow they could see the Kremlin spires – he received word from Sorge and Hozumi that Japan would not attack Russia but move against Britain and the United States, he believed the intelligence. New divisions were transferred rapidly from Siberia to the Moscow front, where

Vyacheslav Molotov, Russian Foreign Minister, signing the non-aggression pact between Soviet Russia and Germany on 23 August 1939, at the Kremlin in Moscow. Standing behind him is his German counterpart, Joachim von Ribbentrop (left), and Josef Stalin (center).

German soldiers in battle during World War II.

they managed to blunt the German assault. Some sources claim Ozaki was such a powerful member of the Japanese war cabinet that he was actually able to influence this decision in Russia's favour. Others have since claimed the Russians used Sorge's spy ring to cover up their own successes in breaking Japanese ciphers.

Sorge was eventually arrested by the Japanese in October 1941. He was never exchanged for a Japanese spy, because both Sorge and the USSR refused to admit that he had been spying for them. It could be argued that Sorge's biggest coup was also his undoing, because Stalin could not afford to let it become known that he had rejected his intelligence data about the German attack in 1941. However, Sorge's efforts were eventually recognised: On November 5, 1964, he was posthumously awarded the honorary title of Hero of the Soviet Union.

BRITAIN FOOLISHLY REJECTS INTELLIGENCE

In other cases, valuable intelligence was rejected for the opposite reason – because it downgraded a threat believed to be far more powerful than it really was. Before the outbreak of World War II, the threat of massive

German bombing raids paralysed potential opponents. Yet London had a prime source of information in retired group captain Michael Christie, who had served as air attaché in Berlin between 1927 and 1930, before the Nazis came to power. Following his retirement, he stayed on in Germany as a businessman. There he used his excellent network of contacts, which included both Hermann Goering, head of Germany's new Luftwaffe, and Erhard Milch, his deputy, to produce regular reports for Sir Robert Vansittart at the Foreign Office on Germany's arms buildup.

One of his prime sources was a German Air Ministry official named Hans Ritter. When the Foreign Office passed on Christie's figures to the British Air Ministry, it demanded to know the source. Christie refused to risk Ritter's life by revealing his name and instead agreed to pass queries and answers back and forth between Germany and Britain. The British Air Ministry saw this as a refusal to cooperate, which made his information suspect, and the ministry continued, for reasons of its own, to magnify the size of the German bomber threat. Their most dramatic assumption: The Luftwaffe could deliver a knockout blow with high explosives, incendiaries and poison gas.

Sir Robert Vansittart, chief diplomatic adviser to the British Foreign Office during World War II.

The German disinformation campaign

The Germans were eager to foster this myth in order to sap the morale of potential adversaries and dissuade them from attacking Germany. They therefore used gullible foreigners, like Charles Lindbergh, to trumpet their message. US intelligence had commissioned Lindbergh in 1938 to assess the threat the German 'Luftwaffe' posed. He therefore traveled repeatedly to Germany, where he toured aviation facilities with the head of the Luftwaffe. Dutifully, Lindbergh announced that the Germans had 10,000 aircraft in service, half of them bombers, that they were turning out 500 planes a month and could triple that output. The real figures concerning German aviation capability, which Christie reported to London, were far more modest – 1,246 bombers out of a total of 3,315 planes, with production running at less than 300 a month.

But almost no one believed him. During the Munich crisis of September 1938, Hitler blackmailed the West into forcing the Czechs to hand over the Sudetenland, where most of their defences were located, leaving the rest of the country open to German invasion a year later. While some members of the Allied authorities, such as Sir Robert Vansittart of the British Foreign Office, were strongly against giving in to Hitler's demands, British and French leaders, terrified by the threat they believed his air force posed, gave him virtually all he wanted. In this Lindbergh again played a part. At the urging of the then US ambassador to Great Britain, Joseph Kennedy, Lindbergh had written a secret memo for the British arguing that if England and France attempted to stop Hitler's aggression at that point in time, it would be military suicide. Although some military historians argue that Lindbergh was basically accurate and that his warnings helped to save Britain from likely defeat in 1938, others argue that in seizing Czechoslovakia and taking over its booming armaments industry, Hitler foiled the last real chance the West had to topple his regime before war began.

NEW INTELLIGENCE PROBLEMS

Today, with fewer channels of information available, mistakes are less likely to happen and disinformation is easier to expose. Problems of interpretation, however, remain, even if they are of a different nature. One such example is the sheer volume of information that must be processed by modern intelligence organizations, which ironically is due to the increased sophistication of the technology available to espionage networks. Intelligence information, therefore, takes longer to reach those who need it. In the graphic American phrase, the ideal intelligence link is 'sensor to shooter'; in other words the shortest and most direct route from the sources who generate the information to the military who can use it to take out the targets it reveals. The longer the delay in getting this information to the relevant people, the greater the risk of the information being out of date even before it can be used.

During the 1991 Gulf War, mobile intelligence units identified Iraqi positions from signals traffic, and as pressure increased, more and more signals were sent in plain language to avoid delays, adding yet more to the information pool. Thus, processing the material took more time. As a comparison, Enigma intelligence sent from Bletchley Park to North Africa in World War II took six hours on average, or three hours at best. Gulf War delays were greater despite the sophistication of the technology.

ESPIONAGE IN ACTION
Pearl Harbor and Ground Zero

America has suffered two catastrophic attacks: the Japanese strike on Pearl Harbour in Hawaii on 7 December 1941, and Al Qaeda's destruction of the twin towers of the World Trade Centre in New York City on 11 September 2001.

Intelligence in both attacks was similar in indicating that some kind of attack was imminent, but the information was too vague to take effective countermeasures. Sharply deteriorating US–Japanese relations in the fall of 1941 made a preemptive Japanese attack likely. But nobody knew where the blow would fall, making it difficult to give priority to Pearl Harbour defences.

Similarly, electronic traffic in the weeks preceding 9/11 intercepted by GCHQ in Britain and NSA in the United States, suggested a major terrorist strike against the American mainland, but again no details about a possible target.

This time, however, the FBI should have been able to put the information it had into a more coherent form. The agency knew, for example, that young Muslims were taking flying lessons without showing any interest in takeoff or landing. Yet none were arrested nor security arrangements improved at major airports or to in-flight security that might have prevented the attack. Even worse, over the previous five years the FBI ignored massive precedent involving hijacked planes crashing into buildings to cause maximum loss of life.

In December 1996 French officials tricked Algerian terrorists into landing a hijacked Air France jet in Marseilles to refuel. Once on the ground the terrorists were killed in a shoot-out. It turned out they had planned to crash the aircraft into the Eiffel Tower. A month later a plot was uncovered in the Philippines to steal an American aircraft and crash it into the headquarters of the CIA at Langley in Virginia. A year after that an Al Qaeda plot to steal a plane from Afghanistan and crash it into the White House was uncovered and foiled. As early as 1998 a plot had

A fiery blast rocks the south tower of the World Trade Center in New York City as the hijacked United Airlines Flight 175 from Boston crashes into the building on 11 September 2001.

been hatched to steal an aircraft, pack it with explosives, and crash it into the World Trade Centre. The authorities also knew of at least seven plots to use airplanes as missiles against airports, military bases, public gatherings and government buildings.

Finally, it now appears that in an attempt to defend the intelligence agencies against accusations of failure, information was leaked in America that the NSA had been given details from GCHQ of two messages from sources in Afghanistan on 10 September that referred to a major operation the following day. However, they were not deciphered until it was too late. Though this was mildly reassuring in that the information was discovered, it was catastrophic in what it revealed to the terrorists. The old intelligence imperative of protecting sources at all costs was ignored, so the chance of picking up warnings of future operations was lost as Al Qaeda moved quickly to tighten security still further.

Satellite image of
Baghdad in 2004.
Satellite imagery is
a vital tool for any
military and
espionage operation
or organization.

NEW TECHNOLOGY SPEEDS THE WAY

When the Americans invaded Afghanistan and Iraq a decade later, things had greatly improved: Use of remotely piloted vehicles (RPVs) controlled from the ground revolutionised intelligence. RPVs could relay target information to other attack units, or sometimes launch onboard weapons themselves, without the need to risk agents' or pilots' lives.

When the British attacked Basra, MI6 agents inside the city identified the Baath party headquarters building, used for a meeting between the city governor and the leaders of Saddam Hussein's forces. They called in an air strike by two US F15s, with British special forces' laser designators guiding the precision bombs to their targets. Though their prime objective – the Iraqi governor nicknamed Chemical Ali – was not killed, he was forced to flee, and the defenses of the city soon collapsed. Wherever possible, the Iraqis used a network of fibre-optic cables to send secure signals between command posts and army units. To force this traffic onto radio networks where it could be intercepted, analysed, and deciphered, special forces teams blew up key junctions in the system.

Mistakes were still made, however. A precision attack on a restaurant where Saddam was supposed to be holding a meeting was thought to have killed him. Not so, as footage of the dictator addressing a crowd in the Mansur district of western Baghdad on 4 April seemed to document, a time when coalition forces were already in the city. Analysts couldn't prove he was dead, but they could cast doubt on whether the footage had been filmed that day. They checked the spy satellite images over Baghdad before and during the fighting and built up a computer-generated 3-D image of the area. They could then compare the weather, the crowds, the vehicles and the state of the buildings with the television pictures of Saddam and establish that a perfect match only existed in early March, two weeks before the war began. Though it did not prove he was dead, it revealed he was not out risking his neck when the fighting was actually in progress.

Finally, following agent reports that Iraqi leaders were meeting in a particular building on 7 April the total delay between producing the information and the first bombs hitting the building was down to an astonishing forty-five minutes. Ironically, this was the alleged time it would take for Saddam's weapons of mass destruction (WMD) to be activated and used – an assumption that would later be proved wrong.

Unmanned surveillance flights are an increasingly important aspect of espionage. Aircraft like this LOCAAS unmanned surveillance vehicle were used in Iraq to survey potential targets without putting human agents in danger.

Using the Information

SPYMASTERS & MASTER SPIES
The WMD That Never Were...

Despite the claims of hidden WMD (Weapons of Mass Destruction), the campaign in Iraq and the occupation of the whole country revealed no traces of such weapons. The claims were based on extensive intelligence work that began in 1995 when Saddam Hussein's son-in-law Hussein Kamil, a former director of the Military Industrialisation Commission that ran the WMD development programs, defected to the West. Efforts intensified in 1998 after UN inspectors departed and the Iraqi regime tightened restrictions and refused to cooperate with the international community. That left intelligence gathering to the UK and the US The Americans led in imaging technology, thanks to its sophisticated satellite systems, but the British had better and higher-placed agents on the ground, including people involved in weapons deployment and in the subversion of the oil sanctions designed to prevent Iraqi WMD development.

The information they unearthed showed that Saddam defied the sanctions and smuggled oil out through Syria, Iran, and Turkey, thus earning cash to buy and develop weapons. That was true, but other information was not. One

British agent, an Iraqi general, claimed – according to Michael Smith, author of *The Spying Game* – in August 2002 that Saddam could prepare and fire his Al-Hussein missile batteries, armed with chemical or biological warheads or the modified Scud missiles, within forty-five minutes. Several plants capable of producing chemical or biological warfare agents had been identified, and it was believed Saddam Hussein could develop a nuclear weapon in under two years.

Making assumptions

It would turn out later that the forty-five-minute rapid-response time was taken from an operating manual for short-range battlefield weapons that assumed they existed and were ready for use. The assumptions – and those

Satellite image of a suspected nuclear facility 380 kilometres northwest of Baghdad, Iraq, taken in December 2000.

Two Iraqi Scud missiles in the back of a tractor trailer secured by US Marines from Task Force Tarawa. The troops found the trailer on a highway in central Iraq on 5 April 2003.

derived from them – proved to be fatally wrong. Iraq was in no position to fire WMD missiles in forty-five minutes, even if it had had them, which it didn't. Nevertheless, the flawed assumption provided a convenient excuse for the Iraq invasion. The uproar of war smothered the details of how firing-time estimates should be defined, a process hamstrung by concern over protecting the sources of that information, and one that became so inflated as to include strategic weapons that did not exist.

The Niger episode didn't help. The CIA passed documents to the UN purporting to show that Saddam had bought uranium in that African country. The documents turned out to be fake and the sale unlikely, according to a report by the American diplomat, Joseph Wilson IV, sent there to investigate. MI6 reportedly had convincing evidence from the French, who had once ruled Niger, and other sources that the sale had taken place, but could not make them public for security reasons. Nor could British and American intelligence confirm a link between Iraq and Al Qaeda, even though their political superiors insisted there had been one, a myth maintained to this day.

Why did they believe in the WMD myth for so long? Because Saddam Hussein needed them to believe it. Without the threat of WMD, he probably would have been toppled from power much sooner, one reason he was willing to risk invasion and almost certain defeat. Survival for Saddam Hussein was ultimately a balancing act between different sets of enemies to maintain his position, his power and ultimately his life.

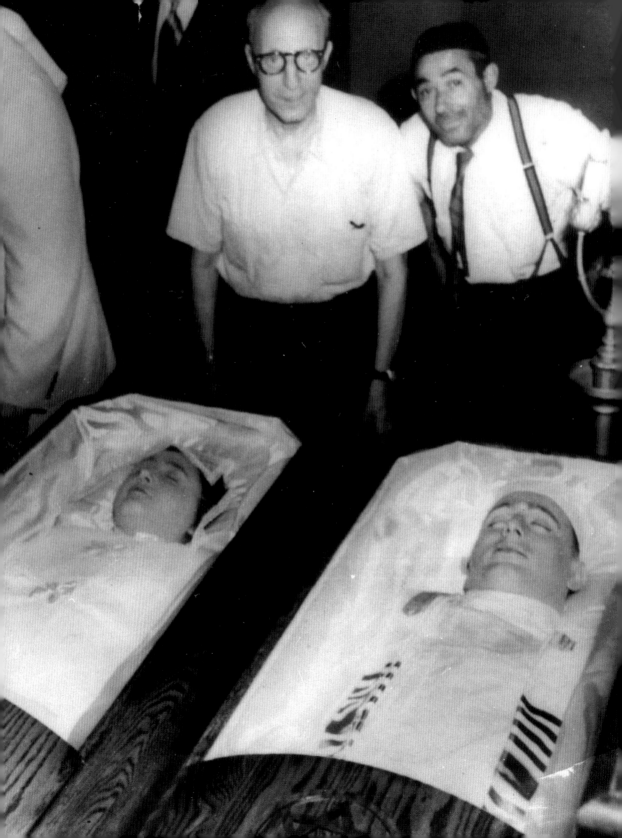

Counterintelligence

Counterintelligence is a vital component in any country's espionage. A counterintelligence service must frustrate the work of enemy agents, penetrate their networks and ensure that the only information sent back to their spymasters is either low-grade data or deliberate disinformation. Counterintelligence agents have some important advantages: They work in their own countries and are unlikely to be captured in enemy territory.

Captured spies have been tortured legally since 1949 because they lack the formal military status that would give them protection from torture under the Geneva Convention. The degree of torture, however, is now questionable as a tool for extracting information; it is now clear that victims will tell their captors whatever their captors want to hear, true or false, to avoid more pain.

Nor is the traditional death penalty for captured spies still necessarily in effect. Captured spies today are often thought to be more valuable as bargaining chips. Each side in the Cold War, for example, considered its own experienced agents as major assets in the intelligence wars. If a good agent is captured, that agent's country will often be willing to trade a captured opposition agent to recover its own spy. There are three reasons for this:

1. A captured and experienced agent might be valuable in a different area of espionage.

2. A captured agent's knowledge of the opposition's methods could be useful for new agents being sent into the area.

3. The idea that a captured agent might be exchanged rather than executed boosts the morale of vulnerable agents working in a challenging and hostile environment.

The bodies of convicted Russian spies Julius and Ethel Rosenberg in the parlour of a Brooklyn undertaker after their execution on 19 June 1953.

Francis Gary Powers, the American pilot shot down in his U-2 plane during a reconnaissance mission over Russia, on trial for espionage in the Great Hall of Columns, Moscow in August 1960.

Searching a captured agent for intelligence

Captured spies are usually searched before questioning, following a set routine. They are watched closely and prevented from speaking to any friends or colleagues arrested at the same time. Smoking, eating, drinking or visiting the toilet are forbidden, and nothing can be thrown away, even what appears to be innocent rubbish, as it may prove to be vital evidence that the captors can use.

In some cases the counterintelligence team may seem to relax its watch and leave the suspect alone. This is to see whether the spy tries to destroy or discard anything. Items carried by the prisoner will also be searched. This will often be done without the prisoner being aware, so that counterintelligence can hide the fact that they may have found something significant or incriminating. In other cases counterintelligence will watch the prisoner's reactions to a search. Apprehension is a danger sign that suggests there is something to find, and sudden relief after the search may tell the searchers that they have missed something.

Any professional spy will try to hide incriminating material as cleverly as possible. For example, messages might be written on silk or cloth and then sewn into concealed pockets in the spy's clothing to avoid the telltale rustling noises of paper. However, searchers often check for hidden material by feeling both sides of a garment at the same time to see if one side is bulkier than the other. Spies may counter this by matching a hidden pocket with padding on the opposite side, but this can be exposed by differences in the thread or stitching between the original tailoring and the entrance to the hidden pockets.

A counterintelligence team also watches for clues in the suspect's body language that may reveal anxiety or relief. Spies, however, often use these giveaway signs to distract a search team by showing anxiety over an article that is completely innocent. Similarly, if the spy's clothing or baggage reveals low-grade sensitive material, like a large amount of currency, for example, the spy may show anxiety when it is found without giving away that there is even more sensitive material still concealed.

After a search, the suspect is usually kept away from others waiting to be searched. If the suspect is released, he or she will be followed very closely (see below) to see where the spy goes and who he or she contacts. The release of a suspect is often followed by that individual's rearrest, together with anyone contacted by the suspect: counterintelligence agencies want to discover the wider espionage network.

Ways of making them talk

Suspects are questioned to get information. Prisoners who are tired and confused lose their concentration and are more likely to betray the truth. To accomplish this, questioners will try to break the suspects' cover stories. To encourage mistakes, questioners will often keep changing the conditions of the prisoner's confinement to undermine resistance levels before the interrogation begins. Sometimes the food will be good; at other times it will be appalling. Sometimes conditions will be relatively comfortable, then treatment will be made much tougher, then relaxed, and so on. Sometimes the prisoner will be left with other prisoners, and at other times they will be left in solitary confinement.

Questioning will start at unpredictable times. At first, the suspect may be asked detailed but nonthreatening questions relating to his or her life and activities well before the arrest. This has two advantages: it induces a state of false security and builds up a wealth of background, so that later more challenging questions can show up half-truths and inconsistencies.

Interrogation techniques

Counterintelligence agents will use a range of techniques to get the information they want. The direct approach – simply asking for the information – may be tried first, especially with junior personnel who may have had little or no resistance training. Alternatively, the interrogators may offer their captive rewards in return for the information. With more experienced agents, subtler forms of questioning are used, such as playing on the agent's emotions by mentioning family members who may be in danger if quesions are not answered. It is therefore vital that agents have training to be able to withstand any of these techniques.

Covert surveillance

Information may be gained by hiding microphones and recorders in suspects' cells. To encourage suspects to talk, they may be left with colleagues between questioning sessions or with agents who seem to be in the same position and who are very outspoken about the stupidity of their captors and how easily they hoodwinked them during interrogation.

When the formal questioning begins, relays of interrogators will alternate friendliness with threats, leave long silences to pressure the detainee to say something, however innocuous, and suddenly go back to earlier answers to look for inconsistencies.

Psychological techniques

Captives may be deprived of sleep for long periods or left in cells that are too hot or too cold. Depriving detainees of watches and clocks to mark the passing of time can help disorient them. Simply being captured will keep prisoners thinking of the circumstances of their arrest. Should they have done anything differently? Were they betrayed? Often, questioners will feed their prisoners' paranoia by claiming that their network was riddled with double agents. Finally, the uncertainty of their ultimate fate will force captives to brood on what the effects of their capture are likely to be.

KEEPING SUSPECTS UNDER SURVEILLANCE

Not all counterintelligence work involves breaking down captured spies. Often, valuable information can result from leaving spies at large and keeping them under surveillance. Provided they remain unaware of being watched, they can reveal links between known agents and other members of their network. Intercepting signals and pinpointing the position of transmitters can help disrupt communications. Regular roadblocks and document checks can intercept supplies of weapons or reveal forged passes

TECHNOLOGY
Spy-proofing a room

Counterintelligence must sometimes be defensive as well as offensive. Whenever people use an office or meeting room to discuss potentially sensitive information, there is always the danger that opposition agents have placed bugs – microphones and links to recording devices – to pick up the conversation. Regular sweeps, using electronic sensors that uncover these devices, are a high-priority insurance against eavesdroppers.

What other kind of checks have to be made? Apart from the obvious , such as always locking filing cabinets and combination safes, counterintelligence agents will look for cameras that may be hidden in spotlights or window openings. They will also search behind radiator pipes for cables that might connect microphones with remote recorders, concealed where they can be retrieved and replaced more easily.

All documents would normally be shredded as a matter of course – not by the relatively simple shredder that cuts a sheet of paper into narrow strips, which could be painstakingly reassembled, but by the crosscut shredders that produce a pile of tiny fragments that complicate attempts to reassemble the material. Finally, printer and electronic typewriter ribbons that are designed for one-time use must be destroyed, because they can be easily read.

The development of modern 'wireless' technology presents new security concerns. Wireless devices transmit information either by radio waves or infrared light, which potentially makes the information sent via that link available to others. Such devices should not be used when transmitting sensitive information.

This Miniphone wiretap kit is used to check for bugs.

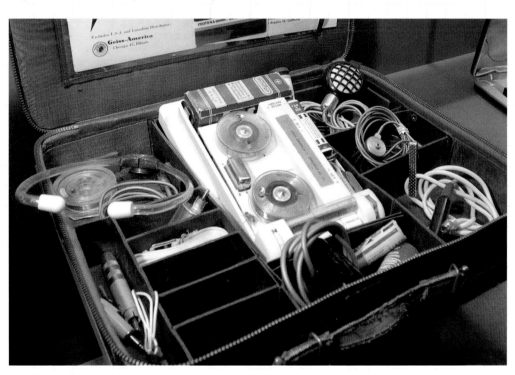

and false identities. Police raids on spy headquarters may capture key agents and valuable information. Some captured agents may be 'turned' to work for counterintelligence against their former comrades and to plant disinformation that will distort the enemy's intelligence picture.

In one respect, counterintelligence will always have the initiative. If counterintelligence agents suspect that there are spies in a sensitive area, they can make all the searches and checks they like. These may fail to directly trap or unmask spies, but sooner or later someone in the spy network will be careless, meet with unexpected bad luck, or make a mistake.

Once an individual is suspected of being a spy – because of being spotted in a sensitive area, such as the vicinity of secret installations or in places already known to be frequented by spies and subagents – he or she will be given a 'tail'. This will usually be a complete team of counterintelligence agents working together to track the suspect – to plot his or her movements and note the locations and people they visit. The value of this information

Police raids on the headquarters of suspected spy organisations can provide key information about the espionage network.

will be greatly increased if the watching can be done without the target knowing.

Tailing a suspect through busy streets

Following someone through a busy city calls for careful planning and quick reactions to unexpected problems or opportunities. Using a full team avoids the danger of having a tail attacked by the suspect without backup. In cases where the suspect is part of a criminal, terrorist or large espionage organisation, a lone tail may be jumped by the suspect's associates.

The single tail. In cases where only one member of a surveillance team has managed to stay with the suspect, that agent has to keep watch until help arrives. The distance between watcher and suspect has to be adjusted for different circumstances. If following the suspect along a busy street, a single watcher will be less conspicuous on the opposite side of the street and behind the suspect. If the suspect turns into a side street, however, the tail will have to race across the intersecting street to see if the suspect enters any of the buildings on the side street. If not, the tail can then turn down the side street in pursuit and remain on the side opposite to the suspect. Unusually crowded areas with multiple exits force a tail to move closer to the suspect to avoid losing contact. Quiet, uncrowded places throw a tail's presence into sharp relief. If a suspect stops to look into a shop window, the tail must find a convincing reason to stop within sight of the suspect long enough for the suspect to start moving again. The tail may have to move ahead of the suspect in plain view and make his or her movements convincing enough to avoid giving away the mission.

The two-person tail. Many problems are avoided with team surveillance. A two-person team allows the first watcher to tail the suspect with a backup watcher in close support, ready to take over when necessary. If the suspect stops to window-shop, for example, the first watcher can walk past and even out of sight, while the second tail stops farther back, ready to go once the suspect starts moving again. Meanwhile, the first tail takes over the fallback position until the next problem arises.

The three-person tail. A three-person operation works best. The first tail stays in close touch with the suspect on the same side of the street, the second tail follows behind and the third tail stays on the opposite side of the street, just behind the suspect. If the suspect turns into a side street, the first tail will walk across the side street and then make the turn, remaining on the

(continued on page 148)

ESPIONAGE IN ACTION
The Venona intercepts

One of the most successful coups of American counterintelligence was the recording and later decryption of Soviet signals from the Soviet consulate in New York and other outstations back to Moscow. These messages provided the first clues to the identities of the Russian spies working within the team responsible for developing the atomic bomb. During the 1940s a huge volume of encrypted traffic sent to Moscow from the Soviet consulate in New York City was picked up and recorded by the US Signals Security Agency. A special unit based at Arlington Hall in Virginia took on the job of decoding the messages and eventually produced a partial but priceless breakthrough.

Their first success resulted from the Finns passing on to the US Office of Strategic Services (OSS) 1,500 pages of a secret Soviet codebook in which individual words, letters, or phrases were each represented by a five-digit code number. President Roosevelt ordered the OSS to return the book to the Russians, but they copied it first. On its own the book was of limited value, because each message was first translated into the series of numbers from the book, but these were then modified by adding to each five-digit code another five-digit number taken from a secret one-time pad (see pages 122–23).

Scientists Lawrence, Fermi and Rabi, who worked on the Manhattan Project researching and developing the world's first atomic bomb.

Provided the senders of the material obeyed the rule to use a different five-digit modifier for each message, the code was virtually unbreakable. But the huge volume of late wartime signals traffic forced cryptographers to use the same combinations more than once. This, together with the huge number of messages being intercepted and recorded, and advice from Soviet defector Igor Gouzenko on Russian code routines and procedures, helped them read some of the messages by the late 1940s.

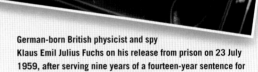

German-born British physicist and spy Klaus Emil Julius Fuchs on his release from prison on 23 July 1959, after serving nine years of a fourteen-year sentence for disclosing nuclear secrets to the Russians.

The Manhattan Project

These messages made it clear that the Soviets had highly placed agents in the most sensitive areas of the US war effort. In particular, they had contacts in the Manhattan Project, where the world's first atomic bombs were being developed. The material, however, referred to these agents only by their code names. The Arlington Hall team therefore had to use other clues in the messages to help them identify the spies.

One message revealed that a spy code-named Charles or Rest was British, and another referred to his sister studying at a US university in 1944. When the analysts consulted personnel records, they found that Klaus Fuchs had fled his native Germany, been given British nationality and sent to work on the Manhattan Project before returning to the United Kingdom to work at the postwar Atomic Energy Research Establishment at Harwell. His sister Kristel had been studying at Swarthmore College in the United States in 1944. MI5 were informed, and they began questioning Fuchs in December 1949. Within a month he had confessed and was given a long prison term.

Though Fuchs did his best to protect the identity of others in his spy network, the decoders eventually identified other code names in the messages – Harry Gold, David Greenglass and eventually, Julius and Ethel Rosenberg. The results of the decoding project, released to the public in 1996 in print and on the Internet, provided a whole new perspective on recent espionage history. In particular, the documents confirmed that despite the furious controversy over their trials, both the Rosenbergs and Alger Hiss had worked for the Russians. The problem during the trials had been that the scientific evidence needed to convict them was at that time thought to be too valuable to be exposed in open court.

In all, only 1 per cent of the 200,000 ciphered signals were read, but those 2,000 deciphered messages – code-named Venona in the United States and Bride in the United Kingdom – proved priceless in spelling out Russian espionage activities in the West. Even more crucially, they eventually yielded the names of many of the spies stealing Western secrets and passing them on to the Soviets.

opposite side of the street as the third tail had done previously. In the meantime, the second tail will take over the first tail's original position behind the suspect and the third tail will take over the second tail's original role. A well-practised team will vary these changes to prevent the suspect from spotting the pattern.

Blending into the background

Watching a professional spy who is trained to spot a surveillance operation in progress may call for a dozen or more surveillance team members, handing the suspect over to one another at frequent intervals to prevent their attentions from becoming too obvious. All members of the surveillance team must blend convincingly into the surroundings. They need clothes appropriate for that particular neighbourhood and for any stores or cafés where the suspect might go. Following a suspect into a bar or restaurant calls for more than the right clothes; it demands enough cash to order drinks or even a meal, and the sense to choose food or a drink that can be finished off quickly if the suspect leaves unexpectedly.

Tricks of the trade

Any objects dropped by the suspect should be picked up out of their field of view. If a suspect steps into a lift, the nearest tail should board the same lift and press the top button, allowing him or her to spot the floor where the suspect gets out. The tail can then either follow the suspect directly or continue to the next floor and resume the tail after descending a flight of stairs. If the suspect stops to use a public telephone, the tail should use an adjacent one, going through the motions of making a call while trying to eavesdrop on the suspect's conversation.

The surveillance team must avoid doing anything to make themselves conspicuous, like making sudden movements when the suspect hails a cab or boards a bus. They must also avoid direct eye contact with the suspect, which makes it more likely that the suspect will recognise the person at a later stage in the operation.

Keeping watch on wheels

Sometimes a suspect may suddenly switch to a vehicle. A professional surveillance team – always aware of this possibility – has a car within easy reach or a member of the team driving behind those on foot, ready to take over at a given signal.

Following a suspect in a car is similar to tailing one on foot. With two cars a surveillance team can switch back and forth to avoid the suspect's noticing

A secret service agent on duty at a railway station in February 1957, looking through a 'spy hole' in his newspaper.

that the same vehicle has stayed in the rearview mirror for a suspiciously long time. In busy city streets, especially those laid out in a regular grid network, surveillance agents have the choice of two methods. The classic parallel technique uses the foot-surveillance method on a larger scale. One surveillance vehicle follows the suspect's car directly, while the second one follows the same course on the next parallel street to one side or the other, ready for the suspect to change direction so it can take up the tail in turn. Alternatively, the second car can stay behind the first, changing places at intervals to avoid too obvious a pattern, in what is called the stacking technique. In other cases, the second car may keep ahead of the suspect so that when called in by the first tracker, it can make a U-turn and approach the suspect from the opposite direction, where it is less likely to be seen as a potential threat.

Surveillance teams can operate at a greater distance from a suspect's car if they can mark it in some way before the chase starts. Police forces will often attach a small transmitter, known as a 'bumper beeper', to the vehicle. This will send out a signal that can be followed by the chase vehicles from beyond the suspect's field of view. At night, when it is more difficult for the suspect to be sure whether a particular car – rather than just any car – is still behind his or her car, the surveillance team may be able to stick a piece of reflective tape to the rear of the suspect's car so they can easily recognise it. The danger, of course, is that the suspect will find the tape at the end of the trip and know that the car has been tailed.

Letting technology take over the chase

Some tracking devices are extremely sophisticated. One open-market unit can be fixed to a suspect's vehicle on the outside for ease of access, but where it will not be too obvious – such as inside a mudguard or under the floorboards. The gadget transmits GPS information when it is triggered by a remote-control command. The GPS information – the current position of the suspect's vehicle to within less than 2.6 m (10 feet), as well as its direction and speed – can be picked up by a computer over the Internet anywhere in the world. Using this GPS gadget, a surveillance team can check a suspect's movements in that vehicle for weeks on end without needing to physically follow them.

Civilian surveillance technology

Many urban areas already contain enough surveillance technology to track a suspect without the need for a surveillance team or specialist technology. For example, video cameras mounted high enough above congested areas to monitor traffic are used to identify licence plates and follow a suspect through a particular area. In large cities like London, congestion-fighting schemes have been introduced by the authorities or are currently under development. Cameras at checkpoints around the periphery of the city take pictures of individual licence plates so that drivers can be identified and billed when they enter the most trafficked centre of the city. Therefore, the system designed to cut down traffic congestion also acts as a sophisticated surveillance system.

Video cameras throughout our towns and cities also provide constant surveillance of people's comings and goings. The latest developments in imaging techniques revolve around computerised monitoring systems. These systems do not observe people directly. Instead, they track their behaviour by looking for particular types of movement, or particular types of clothing or baggage. The theory behind this is that in public spaces people behave in predictable ways. People who are not part of the 'crowd', or anyone behaving suspiciously, do not behave in the same way. The computer can identify their movements and alert the operator that they are acting out of the ordinary. Potentially, waiting in a busy street to meet someone could be enough to trigger this system.

The next generation of road-toll technology will extend to interurban routes and even long-distance highways. On toll roads already, drivers avoid long lines at cash booths by using 'smart' cards that identify them for billing purposes. Eventually, the objective in many countries is to track individual drivers over every trip they make so that they can be charged for entering congested sections of the road network or travelling at particularly busy times of day. Switching from charging drivers for the roads they use and the times they use them, to keeping records of where and when they travel, raises legal questions about privacy issues but needs no radical new technology.

The ever-growing presence of surveillance cameras in our towns and cities means that espionage networks have access to nearly all of our everyday movements and activities.

German U-boats in the Atlantic during World War Two.

For all the German expertise in breaking so many Resistance and SOE networks in occupied Europe during World War II, their judgement failed them in one of the most critical intelligence battles of all. While the Allies were beginning to crack the complex Enigma mechanical cipher system used on land, the German naval Enigma continued to baffle them. Because the huge numbers of possible settings for the cipher wheels and plug-board connections were overwhelming, the only way to break the ciphers was to seize the start setting tables directly from German warships on the high seas.

Operation Ruthless

Commander Ian Fleming, later the creator of James Bond, put forward a dramatic scheme under the code name Operation Ruthless. The idea was to crash a captured German aircraft into the sea at night, carrying agents dressed in German uniforms. They would send out distress signals in German, and when a German rescue vessel turned up, they would seize it, along with its Enigma machine and setting tables. Sadly, as German rescue vessels never operated at night, the plan had to be abandoned. Had it been done in daylight, the Germans might easily have understood the ruse.

Gathering information

Nevertheless, other opportunities occurred in quick succession. On 26 April 1940, a British destroyer, HMS *Griffin*, stopped and boarded a German naval trawler, *Polares*, and seized a bag of coded documents. A year later another British destroyer, HMS *Somali*, crippled a second German trawler, *Krebs*, in Norwegian waters. A boarding party returned with the Enigma settings for the previous month. A month later more documents were seized, from a third German trawler, *München*. This operation was in response to a decrypted Enigma signal giving the positions of a group of trawlers being sent out to transmit weather information back to naval HQs in Germany. The attack on *München* was carried out quickly to reduce the danger of a radio signal being sent, and the ship was taken to a secure anchorage in the Faeroe Islands to avoid the Germans realising she had been captured intact.

Ian Fleming, commander in the British Royal Navy during World War II and the creator of James Bond, was the mastermind behind Operation Ruthless.

Within two days, yet another British destroyer, HMS *Bulldog*, blew the submarine *U110* to the surface by a series of well-aimed depth-charge attacks, but the crew was able to abandon ship because the charges intended to scuttle the submarine failed to detonate. A British boarding party took all the documents they could find, as well as the Enigma machine itself. This enabled the secret-service team at Bletchley Park in England to read German naval messages with relative ease until the code settings were changed again as part of normal procedure at the beginning of June 1941. A cruiser, HMS *Nigeria*, and four destroyers were sent to search for another German weather trawler, *Lauenberg*, in the icy Arctic waters around Jan Mayen Land. They found her on 28 June and opened fire, aiming for near misses to convince the crew to take to the boats.

The final breakthrough

Once again the British took a haul of valuable information before sinking the trawler – having first taken off all her crew. This was the final breakthrough into the German naval Enigma system, and it resulted in a series of successful attacks, including the sinking of German surface supply ships and submarine tankers and the rerouting of convoys to avoid U-boat wolf packs. Even when later modifications, like the adding of a fourth code wheel in February 1942, produced a temporary blackout on German naval Enigma signals, more codebooks were seized from crippled U-boats during the Battle of the Atlantic. Every additional fragment of information helped bring about the ultimate decoding of the impregnable Enigma encryption system.

Yet German faith in Enigma never seriously wavered. After numerous incidents in which Allied aircraft or warships turned up out of the blue to sink German targets, an investigation was mounted by German counterintelligence experts. In each case the complicated mathematics of the Enigma system convinced them that it was still impregnable.

Instead, several other causes were suspected, from spies and saboteurs within the U-boat organisation itself to new Allied direction-finding technologies and equipment. Although these conclusions brought about changes in tactics and operating methods, the true reason for their naval problems was not fully accepted until Germany's final defeat in 1945.

Today's Spies

The context in which spies operate has been transformed over the last two decades. The end of the Cold War has meant a radical switch in techniques, attitudes, personnel and operational methods to match the new enemy – international terrorists whose strong religious ideology, deep contempt for human life (including their own) and culture of secrecy make them formidable opponents. Whatever the real value of the spies of the past, the long-term importance of their new role is paramount.

In the United States the FBI and the CIA were fiercely criticised during the 1970s over civil liberties issues connected with surveillance and telephone tapping. Consequently, the CIA stopped domestic surveillance and the FBI banned wiretaps, searches or surveillance on individuals without warrants. President Ford embargoed assassination operations, and a firewall was built between the CIA (limited to operating overseas) and the FBI (operating only at home). Henceforth, if a foreign suspect was identified overseas by the CIA, that information was given to the FBI only when that suspect actually entered the United States and not before.

This highlights the tension when running spies in a democracy. Even in countries that value freedom and the rule of law, intelligence services have to operate secretly to protect their information sources and avoid revealing to adversaries what is known about them. In addition, facing the brutal realities of international terrorism, agencies have to be able to undertake operations classed as illegal or immoral in the cold light of day but which may be essential to protect the interests of the state and the lives of its citizens. If reined in too closely by official inquiries and overzealous regulators, they may become unable to defend against those wanting to cause them harm. Dictatorships and terrorist organisations face no such dilemmas, but democratic governments must tread the fine line between protecting their citizens' rights and allowing their intelligence operations to work effectively.

Information gathering and analysis continue to play a vital role in espionage work. In 2008, twenty-four additional satellites will be placed in space to increase the area of the globe under observation.

FUNDAMENTALIST TERRORISM

Meanwhile, the last two decades have seen the growth of fundamentalist terrorism around the world. While fundamentalist groups have committed fewer than 10 per cent of terrorist acts in the world, they have accounted for almost 30 per cent of those killed.

Osama bin Laden and Al Qaeda

Al Qaeda is one of the most prominent terrorist groups in operation today. When it was first formed, it had a fairly simple ethos – it was completely opposed to any Muslim regime that did not apply fundamentalist law. Bin Laden himself came to prominence as the backer of the mujahideen, the Islamic guerillas fighting the Soviet forces in Afghanistan after their 1979 invasion. However, he fell out with the most successful resistance leader, Ahmed Shah Mahsood, and sent suicide bombers disguised as a television interview team to murder him.

Holy war

Bin Laden then waged a holy war against the West with the aim to kill as many of their citizens as possible. According to his periodic video communications, his main grievances against the West – and especially the United States – include their support for Israel, their support for several dictatorial regimes in the Middle East and the presence of United States military bases in Saudi Arabia (which the United States abandoned in 2003). Moving from Afghanistan to the Sudan, he set up factories, training camps, and laboratories to develop nuclear and chemical weapons. The first US intelligence success came in 1996 with the defection of Jamal Ahmed Al-Fadl, who claimed to be a high officer in Al Qaeda and had detailed knowledge of their planned operations.

Tracking Al Qaeda

Reacting to his information, the CIA began monitoring Bin Laden and had him expelled from the Sudan in May 1996. He returned to Afghanistan, now controlled by the Taliban, and in June a truck bomb exploded in Saudi Arabia, killing nineteen American service personnel. However, another chink in his security armour opened up in November when the CIA traced his satellite telephone. Over two years GCHQ monitored his calls worldwide through their Morwenstow receiving station in Cornwall.

The calls showed Al Qaeda was structured on the classic cellular plan to reduce damage if agents were caught, with only one person in each cell having any kind of link to, or knowledge of, another cell in the network. It was linked to other terror movements all over the Islamic world, giving them backing and training, and was already planning more strikes against relatively soft Western targets.

Based on the intelligence gleaned from monitoring Bin Laden, by June 1998 the CIA expected attacks on the US mainland – instead, suicide bombers hit US embassies in Kenya and Tanzania on 7 August 1998, killing 224 people. Only a dozen of these were actually Americans; the rest were Africans who had no quarrel with Al Qaeda.

Bin Laden slips through the net

Then the Americans made two mistakes. In addition to ordering a freeze on assets linked to Bin Laden and signing an executive order authorising his arrest or assassination, on 20 August 1998, President Clinton ordered air strikes against a

A Pakistani boy holds up a portrait of terrorist Osama bin Laden, leader of the Al Qaeda network, during a demonstration against the US-led invasion of Afghanistan, on 23 November 23 2001.

pharmaceuticals factory in the Sudan, said to have been built by Bin Laden and used for chemical weapons development. Clinton also targeted one of Bin Laden's training camps in Afghanistan, where military intelligence had apparently indicated a 'gathering of key terrorist leaders' was planned, in an attempt to kill him. Faced with disapproval from some international governments, Clinton stated that he had ordered the attacks not only in response to the embassy bombings but also to preempt more planned terrorist attacks on Americans. However, disappointingly for the United States, the pharmaceuticals factory was said to have been making aspirin, and Bin Laden had left the training camp just six hours before the missiles exploded and destroyed it.

The near miss was so close that Bin Laden must have wondered how the enemy knew his whereabouts so precisely, and he would have suspected insecure communications. Sadly for the Americans, his suspicions were soon confirmed. In the kind of error that gave the Enigma cipher-breakers sleepless nights during World War II, an American official told the media the security agencies were listening to Bin Laden's telephone conversations. Calls on that line ceased, and it was never used again – meaning that the West lost a vital source of information about Al Qaeda.

Picking up the thread

Fortunately, GCHQ could still eavesdrop on other phone lines and intercept faxes sent to Al Qaeda contacts in London. One of them helped with the identification, extradition, conviction and imposition of life imprisonment in the United States for one of the embassy bombers, a Saudi named Mohamed al-Owhali.

By this time these information channels were humming with details of other ambitious plots. These included an Al Qaeda search for nuclear weapons, a plan to crash an explosives-packed aircraft into an American airport with heavy loss of life, a search for volunteers willing to assassinate specific American intelligence agents (a sure sign that the intelligence campaign was damaging Al Qaeda) and plans to kill Western tourists visiting Israel and Jordan to celebrate the approaching millennium. Al Qaeda has also been linked to plans to kill President Clinton during a visit to the Philippines in 1995, and to bomb in midair a dozen US trans-Pacific flights in 1995 – all of which were disrupted or not carried out.

The growing threat

Underlying all these schemes was a determination to mount a major atrocity on American soil. An attempt to bomb Los Angeles International Airport in 1999 was foiled when the leader of the operation was arrested crossing the border from Canada into the United States. A suicide attack on the warship USS *Cole* in Yemen in October 2000 killed seventeen American sailors. In response to this escalating threat, the US government decided to destroy Al Qaeda's training camps in Afghanistan and back the overthrow of the Taliban by the opposition Northern Alliance and thus drive Bin Laden out of his safe haven.

Intelligence officers reported to their government the mounting evidence that Al Qaeda was planning an attack on the United States on its own soil. It was not enough, however, to allow US intelligence to predict the scale, method, dates or targets of the September 11 attacks, in part because of the greater care Al Qaeda took to keep its communications private, and partly because of the politically imposed restrictions under which the CIA had to operate. There was a bar on recruiting agents with criminal records (even if they had the skills or background to get close to the opposition) and an order that the Agency pay all the costs resulting from legal actions in the wake of any operations. Many of these limitations would be removed after September 11, but by then the damage had been done.

How paranoid should we be?

At the time of this writing, there have been no more terrorist attacks in the United States since the attack on the World Trade Centre in 2001. Al Qaeda has chosen softer targets, like nightclubs in Bali, two Muslim wedding parties at a hotel in Jordan (in what may come to emerge as a rare blunder by Al Qaeda itself, because the targets here were fellow Muslims not connected to the Western world or any of their other adversaries) and innumerable bombs, rockets and shootings in Iraq to provoke civil war between the Shia and

Damage caused to USS *Cole* after a terrorist bomb exploded on 12 October 2000 in the port of Aden, Yemen, killing seventeen sailors and injuring approximately thirty-six others.

The rear of the bus that was destroyed by a terrorist bomb in Russell Square, London, during a series of explosions on 7 July 2005.

Sunni. Al Qaeda have also been linked to the 'shoe bomber', Richard Reid, who was arrested on 22 December 2001, for attempting to destroy a passenger airliner by igniting explosives hidden in his shoes, as well as the train bombings in Madrid on 11 March 2004, in which 191 people were killed and nearly 2,000 injured. On 7 July 2005, there were four suicide bomb attacks in the London Underground and aboard a London bus, killing fifty-six people and injuring more than 700. Al Qaeda claimed responsibility, although some believe that the bombers were acting alone.

Video evidence

After attacks such as these, Osama bin Laden released video footage in which he claims responsibility on the part of Al Qaeda and voices his grievances against the West. Experts check each video for clues to the timing of the recording, his location and state of health in the hope that the information will allow troops to track him down, but so far they have been unable to locate and capture him. Some observers suggest that he may already be dead as a result of attacks or from failing health. However, defence against Islamic terrorism remains the top priority for all Western espionage services who now face an enemy more ruthless and lethal than Soviet forces ever proved to be.

ESPIONAGE FOR COMMERCIAL GAIN

Spies are increasingly being used against industrial and commercial targets. Governments monitor the economic health of newly industrialised countries and watch for signs of unrest and political instability. In addition, countries subject to sanctions or other restrictions are watched to ensure they are not avoiding these measures, building up armaments or retaliating by sponsoring terrorist groups.

Big-brother technology

US Keyhole and Lacrosse intelligence satellites use infrared technology to see through darkness, bad weather, or even camouflage and can gather photographic and radar imagery as well. In 2008 these will be replaced by a highly secret array of twenty-four smaller satellites under the Future Imagery Architecture plan. These satellites are more mobile and positioned farther out in space to increase the area of the globe under observation at any moment. The new system promises to deliver much more data, with shorter gaps between transmissions. Imagery from satellites and reconnaissance aircraft (including RPVs) can be fed to ground-based computers to generate enhanced 3-D pictures of a given area and identify standard installations and pieces of equipment.

In Britain the Defence Intelligence Staff (DIS), created in 1964 when the three armed forces merged their intelligence services, is responsible for gathering and assessing intelligence concerning military threats to the UK and its allies. It monitors weapons, capabilities, tactics, order of battle, personalities of key commanders and the loyalty and morale of armed forces personnel of a hundred countries worldwide. It also checks economic, political and scientific information on defence-related issues, together with technology transfer, arms sales and defence industries. Finally, it monitors compliance with arms-control agreements and signs of the proliferation of NBCD (Nuclear, Biological, and Chemical Defense) weapons.

The French play dirty

At present the French seem to be both the greatest complainers and the greatest users of commercial espionage. Though they fiercely criticise the sharing of information between Britain and the United States, they have been highly successful on their own. The SDECE (Service de Documentation Exterieure et de Contre-Espionage), the French equivalent of Britain's MI6 (and to some extent the CIA), found out about US plans to devalue the dollar in 1971 and warned the French Treasury, which made vast profits on the international currency market.

With the election of Francois Mitterand as president in 1981, the SDECE was renamed the DGSE (Direction Generale de la Securite Exterieure). Mitterand appointed Pierre Marion, former head of Air France, as its director, and he claimed that agents managed to fix microphones in the seats of Air France aircraft to record the conversations of foreign business passengers – information that enabled the French to undercut the Americans and the Russians to win a billion-dollar contract to supply India with Mirage fighter bombers.

On another occasion two agents of the French consulate in Houston, Texas, were accused of stealing the contents of garbage containers from outside the headquarters of Texas Instruments. They denied it when questioned by the FBI, though the CIA later obtained a secret French file listing their agents' highest-priority targets among American and British firms. They included Boeing and IBM as well as Texas Instruments, and also Ferranti, Vickers, Westland and British Aerospace.

The United States fights back

Nevertheless, the Americans are not passive victims. The NSA (the US National Security Agency, responsible for espionage, counterintelligence and surveillance) monitored details of the huge Al Yamamah contract for Britain to supply Saudi Arabia with £50 billion (US$90 billion) of military equipment, including Tornado fighters and bombers, ironically using its British base at Menwith Hill to do the eavesdropping.

More actively, France accused the United States of actually stealing a contract with the Saudis for French companies to supply warships and airliners. In another case, they maintain that the United States attempted to replace a French company supplying the Brazilians with a satellite surveillance system. According to the DGSE, the mistress of a French official at the GATT (Global Agreement on Tariffs and Trade) talks was exposed as a CIA agent, charged with persuading that official to reveal details of the French negotiating position.

Weapons trade

Other prime espionage targets in the commerce of the post-Cold War world

include Russia's attempt to overcome economic weakness. With her soldiers paid poorly, irregularly or not at all, local military commanders were pressed to raise cash by selling weapons, from AK47s up to missiles and nuclear materials. The problem now is one of distribution, because countries and even terrorist groups could get their hands on weapons of mass destruction.

US Secretary of Defence Donald Rumsfeld and Prince Sultan, Saudi defence minister, meeting through an interpreter (centre) after the September 11 terrorist attacks on the United States.

OPENING THE FILES
The end of the Cold War opened up secret files kept behind the Iron Curtain. They have replaced speculation with facts, at least in part. For example, the American Communist Party tried to portray itself as American first and Communist second, owing its primary allegiance to US interests. However, Russian documents show that the party put Soviet interests first, for example by recruiting Americans to serve as Russian agents.

The truth about the Venona signals
The files also contained more details of Western operations, like the deciphering of the Venona signals (see pages 144–45). The signals revealed compelling – and damning – evidence against the Rosenbergs, Harry Gold and Alger Hiss, which, however, had not been presented at their trials

President Franklin D. Roosevelt speaking with Harry Hopkins, who was later accused of being a Soviet agent by former KGB chief Pavel Sudoplatov.

for security reasons. Failure to do so left doubt about their guilt or innocence and allowed Hiss supporters to depict the trial as a right-wing witch hunt.

Sometimes the truth remains hidden

Even now secrets and lies remain, some in the public domain. KGB chief Pavel Sudoplatov was the former head of the counterintelligence section responsible for killing enemies of the Soviet Union and masterminding the assassination of Leon Trotsky with an ice pick in Mexico in 1940. His memoirs included dubious claims about the achievements of his team and of the KGB in general, including details of many Soviet intelligence operations carried out over the course of his career. He also claimed that several high-profile Western politicians and scientists were in fact Soviet spies. For example, he insisted that Harry Hopkins, wartime adviser to President Roosevelt, was a Soviet agent, as was J. Robert Oppenheimer of the Manhattan Project for developing the first US nuclear weapons. Neither claim has ever been substantiated, nor was it suspected at the time.

MODERN TRAITORS AND THEIR MISTAKES

Few spies make as brazen mistakes as Boyce and Lee, but given the pressures agents work under, some mistakes are inevitable, no matter how professional the spy. Psychology plays a role. Some develop a sense of invulnerability after years of passing out information successfully and receiving lucrative payments. Even the most highly motivated agent with years of espionage experience, like Oleg Penkovsky (see pages 46–47), could prove astonishingly careless – he kept photos of himself wearing British and American military uniforms in his Moscow apartment. Others fall prey to temptations resulting from the money they make from their spying activities.

The greedy spy

Master spy John Walker's US Navy experience brought him salable information and the habit of following routines carefully. His Russian handlers supplied instructions for exchanging information and payments: He was to leave photographs in a trash bag beside a country road and mark the spot with an empty soft-drink can. The Russians would then drop his payment in another bag, also marked with a can, but on a different route.

Precautions like this enabled Walker to spy for seventeen years, ten times as long as Boyce and Lee. He was confident enough to recruit his wife, son, elder brother and friend into a highly successful and lucrative business. But finally he too made a fatal mistake. He used the money to fund affairs and then abused his wife to the point where she warned the authorities, even though she herself was involved. She contacted the FBI, and Walker only realised something was wrong when he went to pick up a KGB payment and found it was missing.

Later a Soviet defector, Vitaly Yurchenko, revealed that the cipher information the Walkers had provided had enabled the KGB to read more than a million messages. Among the data was information that enabled the Russians to make their submarines much quieter and more difficult to follow and identify.

The careless drunk

Perhaps the most dangerous spies of all, especially in recent times, have been those changing loyalties from within the West's own espionage and intelligence organisations. Aldrich Ames was the son of an agent in the CIA, who himself joined the Agency in 1962 at the age of twenty-one. By 1985 he was selling secrets to the Russians from within the CIA's counterintelligence branch. This involved names and details of CIA double agents. These were Soviet citizens working for the United States who were tracked down by the

(continued on page 168)

THE FALCON AND THE SNOWMAN
A Tale of Two Amateurs

Christopher Boyce and Andrew Daulton Lee were two of the most naïve agents in the history of espionage, and among the most colourful, as Robert Lindsey's 1979 book *The Falcon and the Snowman* attests. Boyce and Lee were childhood friends in California. They drifted apart in high school, where Lee became a drug dealer, while Boyce was an A student.

By the time Boyce reached college, however, he was adrift. He dropped out of three schools until his father, a retired FBI agent, found him a job with TRW, a major defence contractor working on satellite systems for the CIA. Boyce was twenty-one years old when he started work in 1974. He had shucked the faith of his Catholic boyhood, become disillusioned by Vietnam and the United States inspired ouster of Chilean president Salvador Allende, and decided to pass some of the classified material that passed through his hands at work to the Russians – for cash.

He now contacted his boyhood friend. Lee was always in need of cash to feed his drug habit. He already had a criminal record, had spent time in jail, pondered turning informer but decided against it, fearing his partners in crime more than the authorities. At first Lee hesitated, but then he agreed to act as Boyce's courier. In April 1975 he showed up at the Soviet embassy in Mexico City offering to sell secrets. The official he met, Vasily Okana, was dubious – Lee had walked into the embassy without taking any precautions – but when he looked over the wares Lee was carrying, he realised they were the real goods – among them a computer card from the National Security Agency (NSA) crypto system.

Playing the game

Complex arrangements for meetings outside the embassy followed, complete with code words and other insignia. Two strips of adhesive tape were stuck in a cross on pylons carrying power cables or telephone wires to arrange meetings at prearranged locations, like a restaurant or night club.

Boyce, meanwhile, had little trouble getting the information the Russians wanted. Security at TRW was lax. The spy had little trouble penetrating the 'black vault' where secrets were kept and had even less of a problem bringing them out of the plant. Employees made regular 'booze' runs, so when Boyce walked by the guards with a satchel full of documents, the guards paid him little heed. When documents had to be returned, he hid them in the soil of a potted plant in order to smuggle them back into the building. The copies and the computer materials were given to Lee, who set off for Mexico.

The Russians paid well, and things moved smoothly. But then Lee began to take a larger and larger slice of their cash. In the end Boyce ended up with $20,000 only. Lee used the money to buy heroin, and as his addiction grew, so did his carelessness. He boasted about being a spy, a boast no one took seriously – except for Boyce, who feared that Lee would tell his father and that his father would turn in his son.

The final meeting

Boyce began to pull back from espionage. The Russians made demands he could not meet because the material was not in the 'black vault' and was therefore inaccessible. He developed other interests and was going back to college to study history and political science. He thought he might move to Russia. He gave his notice to TRW but decided on one last coup – photographs of TRW's design for the 'Pyramider', a CIA spy satellite.

Unfortunately, Lee made for the embassy without arranging a meeting place. When the guards refused to let him in, he scribbled 'KGB' on a pocket dictionary and threw it over the embassy wall. He was grabbed by an undercover squad of Mexican police, who were posted there after an antigovernment terrorist had thrown a suspicious package over the same wall. Lee was taken to a police station and searched, and his identity and intentions were exposed. He was tortured by Mexican authorities, who were convinced he was involved in the murder of a local policeman. Eventually he was returned to the United States to be investigated and charged.

The trial

The trail led back to Boyce, and when both men were put on trial in separate hearings, they claimed they had been working as double agents for the CIA to plant false information

Convicted spy
Chirstopher Boyce being escorted from the
federal courthouse by US marshals on his way to jail.

on the Soviets. This claim was discredited, and Lee was sentenced to life imprisonment; Boyce got forty years. He escaped three years later and went on the run for more than a year and a half, following a second career as a small-time bank robber while taking flying lessons. He intended to buy, borrow, or steal a light aircraft in Alaska and fly to a new life in the Soviet Union. In this too he was unsuccessful. He was spotted, captured and returned to prison to serve out his sentence.

This still shot from an FBI video shows Aldrich Ames, Moscow's master spy inside the CIA from 1985 to 1994, walking through a shopping mall on his way to meet a Soviet contact.

KGB using Ames's information and then imprisoned or executed. One of those he betrayed was Oleg Gordievsky, who had been head of the KGB's operations in London before returning to Moscow. His London handlers warned him in time, and MI6 brought him West before he could be arrested.

Ames was well paid for his services and used the money to live in luxury. He acquired a house and a car, took expensive trips and bought lavish gifts. He explained his extravagant lifestyle by pointing to the family fortune of his Colombian wife. In the end, carelessness over money, heavy drinking and mistakes at work brought him under suspicion. To avoid frightening him into defecting, CIA agents searched the rubbish left outside his house and put it all back carefully to disguise signs it had been tampered with. Ultimately they found the evidence they needed – a ribbon from a one-time computer printer that showed incriminating messages. He and his wife, who had helped Ames, were arrested in 1994, and he was sentenced to life imprisonment, mainly for causing the deaths of at least ten agents.

A dead letter drop too far

In early 2001 it was the FBI's turn to suffer embarrassment at the hands of an insider: Robert Hanssen. He was more careful than Ames, salting away huge payments from the Russians. He maintained high security, arranged his own dead drops and remained a Russian agent for at least seventeen years. He was even given details of ongoing FBI investigations as part of his work in the Bureau, which made it almost impossible to catch him unawares.

Finally he was betrayed by the one factor outside his control. The loss of US agents to the Russians suggested a Russian mole inside the FBI. Only a limited number of people within the Bureau had access to the kind of information being leaked to the SVR (Sluzhba Vneshnei Razvedki, or Foreign Intelligence Service, and the successor to the KGB), and finally suspicion fell on Hanssen. He was placed under surveillance in 1997: a homing device was put on his car and his computer was tapped. After more than three years' searching, agents spotted him making a dead letter drop in February 2001, and he was arrested and sentenced to life imprisonment.

TUNNEL VISION – SUCCESS OR FAILURE FOR OPERATION GOLD?

One particular episode demonstrates the difficulty of finding the truth about espionage operations. Two Western intelligence coups, code-named Silver and Gold, involved digging tunnels in jointly occupied cities across zone borders to tap into Soviet telephone lines carrying political and military information. Because little of this material was sent by radio, this gave Western spies a valuable window into Soviet plans, decisions, and intentions.

Vienna to Moscow

The first of these was mounted in Vienna, then under four-power Allied occupation, in autumn 1948. From Soviet headquarters in the old luxury Hotel Imperial, underground cables carried messages to Moscow, to the satellite government in Prague, and to all the Russian military units in their occupation zone. This was priceless information, and because the borders between the different zones were so irregular, the cables ran beneath the British zone of the city in several places – so MI6 decided to tap them.

This involved a series of short tunnels from properties lining the major routes under which the cables ran. The Austrian Post Office revealed that cables under the Aspangstrasse carried Soviet military signals and contained points where soldered joints had been made and where a tap could therefore be made undetected. Unfortunately, heavy goods vehicles driving along the Aspangstrasse from nearby railway yards caused the roadway to dip above the tunnel, and workmen turned up to investigate. But by involving the Austrians, the tunnel was maintained until 1951, when the Russians changed their cable routes. Even then, three other tunnels continued delivering vital intelligence until the occupying troops finally left Austria in 1955 and the operation, by now involving the CIA as well as MI6, was closed down.

A Russian soldier standing in a newly discovered tunnel on 26 April 1956. The Russians claimed that the tunnel, which stretched from West to East Berlin, was used to tap Soviet phone lines.

The Berlin tunnel

Meanwhile, after the Venona interception of radio signals (see pages 144–45), the Russians transferred their most sensitive signals in Berlin from radio to underground cables for added security. The only way to break into this traffic was to dig another tunnel, this time from the US occupation zone to the cables linking KGB headquarters in Karlshorst and Soviet Army headquarters at Zossen to the south of Berlin. Agents in the East German telecommunications service told the CIA the best sites for tapping the cables, and a tunnel was dug from Rudow in the US sector for 548 m (600 yards) into the Soviet sector to reach the cables. This meant shifting 3,000 tonnes of soil in a much bigger operation than the Vienna tunnels.

The new tunnel was dug from inside three specially constructed warehouses posing as equipment storage for the US forces in the city and was later camouflaged as a radar site. One had a particularly large and deep basement, partly for the spoil from digging the tunnel. The other two held digging teams and equipment, along with experts who recorded and processed the information once the taps were in place.

Nothing showed outside, and security was extremely tight. The West Germans were not told, with the US paying most of the $6 million cost. This was another joint US/UK operation. British expertise was used for the actual tapping and in the final approach to the cables themselves, which were buried just 60 cm (2 feet) underneath the Schonefelder Chaussee, a very busy route.

Because of sandy subsoil, the tunnel had to be built like the London Underground, assembled section by section as the digging progressed, and sealed by concrete forced into the gap between the steel tube sections and the surrounding soil. Finally the cable had to be approached from below, up an accurately sited vertical shaft. This could only be positioned by placing an object as close to the spot as possible and using a range finder from the Allied side to measure the distance.

Several times a softball was thrown to the right spot, but the East German guards picked it up each time and obligingly threw it back. Finally, a US service truck was sent to break down on the Schonefelder Chaussee. While repairs were being made, one of the crew put down a special reflector that enabled the distance to be measured precisely. When the tap was in place, it was so close to the surface that the footsteps of patrolling border guards could be clearly heard.

By this time the KGB already knew about the tunnels. MI6 agent George Blake, a naturalised Briton serving in the wartime Royal Navy who had been recruited into intelligence work in 1947. He was working in the British Legation in Seoul, capital of South Korea, at the start of the Korean War. North Korean forces overran the city and the diplomats were sent to a prison camp in Manchuria for harsh treatment and attempts at brainwashing. In April 1953 Blake was repatriated to Britain and rejoined intelligence with fulsome praise for not having disclosed sensitive information to his captors. However, he nursed a deadly secret. During his captivity, he had become a Communist and been recruited as a KGB double agent.

First he passed material to the Soviets showing the detailed and accurate information obtained through tapping the Vienna cables. Later he attended meetings to plan the whole Berlin tunnel operation and was able to alert his Soviet controllers.

Nevertheless, the taps gave Western intelligence details of KGB and satellite secret-service operations, as well as valuable military information. The whole operation was nearly blown on one occasion when the ground was covered by a thin layer of snow, and the heat of the equipment operating within the tunnel was melting the snow above it. Only by installing refrigeration units to bring the temperature down could they avoid its course being revealed to the Russians. In all, it operated for eleven months, until severe

Portrait of double agent George Blake, issued by Britain's Scotland Yard after his escape from Wormwood Scrubs prison in October 1966, where he was serving a forty-two-year sentence.

flooding in east Berlin caused the authorities to undertake cable repairs. By tapping telephone conversations, the Allies knew exactly when excavation teams would arrive to examine the tapped cables and were able to withdraw well before the final discovery of the tunnel, in the spring of 1956.

Although the Russians later claimed that Blake's warnings had led them to use the cables as a channel for disinformation to mislead the West, the truth seems to have been they were loath to reveal they had been outwitted, and even more reluctant to give away their mole in the West who had access to this highly secret operation. Even the arrival of the cable maintenance teams and the discovery of the tunnel seems to have been a routine operation, and not action initiated by Blake's betrayal.

This was confirmed at meetings between former chiefs of Eastern and Western intelligence in Berlin in 1993, when Blake's former controller and head of the KGB in Germany, Sergei Kondrashev, confirmed his service had kept the Soviet armed forces in the dark about the cable tapping to protect their agent and the other valuable information he was providing. Blake himself was finally identified by the defector Michael Goleniewski, deputy head of Polish counterintelligence, as the undercover agent referred to by the KGB as 'Lambda 2'. He was arrested, tried, and sentenced to forty-two years in prison in 1961 but five years later was sprung from Wormwood Scrubs prison in London. He was spirited away to Moscow in a triumphant coup, which in Soviet eyes partially made up for humiliation over the tunnel.

LETTERS OF THE LAW

One enduring contradiction in the world of espionage has been the contrast between the shameless eavesdropping on other countries' diplomatic communications and the idea that opening mail addressed to others remains outside the limits of the conduct to be expected of gentlemen. While laws were drawn up in most countries to guarantee the confidentiality of postal services, governments routinely flouted their own regulations to keep abreast of what enemies and their intelligence services might be up to.

The British and the Austrians, in particular, conducted mail-tampering on an assembly-line basis, steaming open letters before reading and resealing them and forwarding them to their destinations. Replacement seals were made to disguise any sign of a letter being opened and copies made of sensitive information contained within. Yet it was revolutionary regimes like France and the fledgling United States that turned their backs on this tactic with the greatest fervour.

Since then, bans on mail tampering have alternated with laws allowing the practice to continue with certain safeguards. In Britain a government warrant was needed to open another's letters. In the United States diplomatic mail was opened when thought necessary, but private mail was mostly left alone. Only now, under the imperatives of the current war on terror, has President Bush made it possible for the National Security Agency to eavesdrop on the communications of private citizens. While this seems to fly in the face of previous laws and guarantees under the banner of preventing future terrorist atrocities, in essence it merely reveals what has been going on in most countries at different times throughout the history of espionage.

DON'T KNOCK THE ROCK

One recent Russian–British flare-up is a clear indication that espionage did not cease with the end of the Cold War. The Russians complained that British diplomats in Moscow had been communicating with Russian prodemocracy organisations seen as subversive by the increasingly authoritarian Putin administration. The evidence included a counterfeit rock left by a path in a Moscow park, which was filled with electronic equipment as a sophisticated dead letter drop. Instead of physically dropping a message for a later pickup, an agent could walk past the rock carrying an unobtrusive handheld device that transmits information to the rock's internal memory. Another agent could then pick up the information using another electronic device.

The technology is designed to minimise chances that counterintelligence spot the agent. Nevertheless, the Russians had photographs that apparently show British diplomatic staff kicking the rock (possibly to stir it into life) and then removing it altogether. So far no official expulsions have taken place and British denials have been muted, though Russians have been arrested for collaborating with the British. Experts consider the whole exercise to be aimed at cutting off British backing for some of the prodemocracy groups.

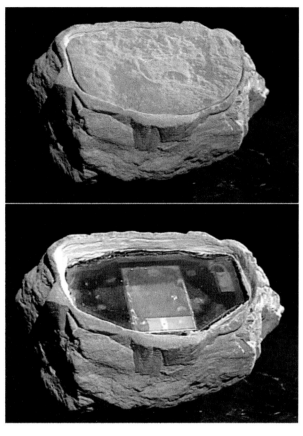

Electronic equipment concealed in a rock in a park outside Moscow, which the Russian authorities claimed was used by four British embassy staff members to receive intelligence provided by Russian agents. This device was discovered in January 2006.

Index

175

Picture credits and acknowledgements

The publishers would like to thank the following for permission to reproduce images.
Getty Images: pp. 8, 10, 17, 18, 19, 20, 21, 24, 26, 27, 29, 30, 32, 34, 36, 41, 50, 52, 55, 56, 59, 62, 68, 74, 76, 81, 82, 84, 85, 85, 88, 90, 92, 94, 95, 97, 105, 108, 110, 115, 118, 122, 129, 130, 133, 137, 147, 149, 157, 159, 160, 163, 164, 167, 168, 170, 171, 173; Rex Features: pp. 33, 39, 60, 64, 71, 72, 91, 116, 143, 153; TopFoto: pp. 12, 43, 46, 47, 58, 93, 104, 107, 117, 119 (bottom), 121, 128, 131, 135, 138, 140; Science Photo Library: pp. 15, 22, 67, 70, 98, 111 (top), 112, 126, 136, 144, 146, 151, 154; Science & Society Photo Library: pp. 101, 119 (top); Photolibrary: pp. 48, 154; akg-images: p. 40.